# Festivals

# Festivals

Compiled by

RUTH MANNING-SANDERS

*Illustrated by*
RAYMOND BRIGGS

E. P. Dutton & Co., Inc.   New York

74 171

Acknowledgements for copyright material appear on pp. 187–188.

First published in the U.S.A. 1973 by E. P. Dutton & Co., Inc.
Text compilation copyright © 1972 by Ruth Manning-Sanders
Illustrations copyright © 1972 by William Heinemann Ltd.

ISBN: 0-525-29675-1   LCC: 72-78084


Printed in Great Britain
by Cox & Wyman Ltd., London, Fakenham and Reading

First Edition
T 71639

# Contents

5

January

# JANUARY 1st

## New Year's Day

> The merry year is born
> Like the bright berry from the naked thorn.
> *Hartley Coleridge*

The word January comes from the name of a Roman god, *Janus*, which again is derived from the Latin word, *janus*, a gate or opening. All the gates of ancient Rome were held to be under the care of Janus; and because through gates there is both a going out and a coming in, the god was represented as having two faces, one looking forward, one looking back. And that is perhaps what we all do on the first day of the year; for, as William Hone says in his *Every-day Book*, 'The man who does not at least *propose* to himself to be better this day than he was last, must be either very good or very bad indeed.'

> The old year now away is fled,
> The new year it is enteréd,
> Then let us now our sins down tread
> And joyfully all appear.


> Let's be merry this holy day,
> And let us run with sport and play,
> Leave sorrow, let's cast care away.
> God send you a happy new year.

And now with new year's gift each friend
Unto each other they do send,
God grant we may our lives amend,
And that the truth may appear.

Now like the snake cast off your skin
Of evil thoughts and wicked sin,
And to amend this year begin.
God send you a merry new year.

*14th century carol*

## Some Old New Year Customs

The giving of presents on New Year's Day is a time-old custom which has now almost entirely dropped out. During the reign of Queen Elizabeth I, the custom of presenting New Year's gifts to the sovereign was carried to an extravagant length. The Queen's wardrobe and jewellery must have been principally supplied from her New Year's gifts. The Earl of

Leicester's New Year gifts (1571) exceeded those of any other nobleman: 'one armlet, or shakell of gold, all over fairely garnished with rubyes and dyamondes, haveing in the closing thereof a clocke, and in the forepart of the same a fayre lozengie dyamonde without a foyle, hanging thereat a round juell fully garnished with dyamondes, and perle pendant, weying 11 oz: in a case of purple vellate all over embroidered with Venice golde, and lyned with greene vellat.'

The first person to cross the threshold after midnight on December 31st was called the *first-foot* or *lucky-bird*. In most parts of Scotland he should be a fair-haired man; in most parts of England he should be dark-haired. Often one person would act as a first-foot for many houses, getting a shilling at each. In Stafford the sweep with his brushes, and wearing a top-hat, was the village first-foot, because he was the darkest man in town. He entered through the front door, shook hands with everybody, wished them a happy new year, and went out through the back door.

When all the family and their friends were gathered round the supper table on New Year's Eve, a bowl of spiced ale was brought in. From this bowl the head of the family drank the health of each of the company in turn, saying as he did so '*Waes-hail*!' (be in good health). The bowl was then passed round that all might drink, each person, as he raised the bowl to his lips, answering '*Drink-hail*!' Hence the bowl from which they drank came to be known as the *Wassail Bowl*.

Meanwhile the poorer people went round from house to house, carrying an empty bowl decorated with ribbons, collecting money and singing. This was called 'Going a-wassailing'. Groups of children, too, went a-wassailing. And here is their song:

> Here we come a-wassailing
> Among the leaves so green,
> Here we come a-wandering,
> So fair to be seen.

*Love and joy come to you,*
*And to your wassel too,*
*And God send you a Happy New Year,*
*A New Year,*
*And God send you a Happy New Year!*

We are not daily beggars,
That beg from door to door,
But we are neighbours' children,
Whom you have seen before.

We have got a little purse,
Made of stretching leather skin,
We want a little of your money,
To line it well within.

God bless the master of this house,
Likewise the mistress too,
And all the little children
That round the table go.

Good master and mistress,
While you're sitting by the fire,
Pray think of us poor children,
Who are wandering in the mire.

*Love and joy come to you,*
*And to your wassel too,*
*And God send you a Happy New Year,*
*A New Year,*
*And God send you a Happy New Year!*

# A Chinese Boy's New Year

## *E. F. Lattimore*

The Old Year was getting tired, and it was going away soon. That was what Wu's mother told Wu and Su-lan. As soon as the Old Year had left, the New Year would be here. That would mean a holiday, and gifts for every one.

'And firecrackers!' said Wu.

'Yes, firecrackers, too,' said his mother.

Wu remembered how it had been last year at New Year's time. His brothers had all come home, bringing strings of firecrackers. They had also brought fireworks – the kind you light at night. Then they shoot up into the sky, where they make beautiful pictures.

'Will my brothers come home this New Year and bring firecrackers?' asked Wu.

'I think so. They have always come before,' said his mother.

During the last days of the Old Year everyone was busy. Special food had to be cooked, new clothes must be finished.

Bright lanterns were taken down from the shelves in the storeroom, each with a candle inside it, waiting to be lighted. These would be hung in the garden to welcome the New Year in, and Wu and Su-lan could help to light them when the time came. There were other preparations, though, that they were not allowed to take part in. Their mothers talked in whispers whenever the children were near.

'They are going to give us presents,' said Su-lan to Wu. 'And we must give them presents, too.' Wu looked worried. What presents could he give?

Su-lan had hemmed handkerchiefs for her mother and for Wu's mother, one red and one green, since gay colours suited the New Year best. But Wu did not know how to sew, and he did not know what to make. If only he had some money, so he could buy some presents! . . . Each morning he felt in his pocket, and each morning it was empty. Wu wished he could find a hundred pennies in it!

'Why do you look so sad, Wu?' the gardener asked him, as Wu stood watching him sweep the snow from the garden.

'I haven't any money,' said Wu. 'And I want to buy presents.'

'Well,' said the gardener, 'why don't you earn some money?'

Wu had never thought of trying to earn money before.

'It is easy,' said the gardener, handing him his broom. 'Here! You can sweep the garden for me, and I will give you two pennies.'

Wu's face lighted up in a smile. Two pennies!

When the garden was swept, and two pennies jingled in Wu's pocket, he wondered how he could earn some more money.

'The cook may give you some work to do,' suggested the gardener. So Wu set forth to the kitchen to talk to the cook.

The kitchen was a very busy place these days. Besides preparing the ordinary meals, the cook was making New Year's cakes, and his hands were covered with flour. On the stove

15

there was soup that needed to be stirred, but when he stirred it with the ladle, the handle got covered with flour.

'I have earned two pennies,' Wu said to the cook.

'You can earn another,' the cook said. 'Stir this soup for me, and I will give you a penny.'

Wu stirred the soup very carefully, and it neither spilled nor stuck to the pot. 'That is fine!' said the cook. 'Here is your penny!'

Three pennies! But Wu wanted still more pennies to add to the three that were stored in his pocket. The next person to give him work was Su-lan's mother. He helped her dust the furniture in Tai-Tai's sitting room, and she gave him a penny. Tai-Tai gave him two more.

Now Wu had six pennies. He showed them to his father, and his father said, 'I am very pleased that you know how to earn money. Some day, I hope, you will be a gatekeeper like me. If you watch the gate for a while now, I will give you *ten* pennies.'

Wu was very glad to watch the gate for a while! He sat outdoors on his father's stool, with Ding (the dog) for company. Visitors called to see the master and mistress of the house, bringing New Year's greetings and little gifts. Some of the callers Wu knew, and he asked them to come in. Others, who were strangers, he told to wait a moment. Then he went into the gatehouse and spoke to his father, and his father decided whether the strangers could come through the gate or not.

Watching the gate was important work. It was cold work, too. But Wu felt warm, thinking of all the pennies he had earned. They seemed to jump around in his pocket, wanting to be spent, and Wu kept wondering what he could buy with them.

Some new person must be drawing near, for Ding began to bark. Wu saw a man coming down the road, carrying two blue bundles. Wu recognized him at once, for it was the pedlar – the very same pedlar who had come before.

16

'I have fine wares for the New Year!' the pedlar was singing. When he saw Wu, he said, 'Have you any money today?'

'Yes!' cried Wu, 'Oh yes!' He ran to tell his father that the pedlar had come by with fine things for the New Year.

'We don't want anything,' said his father. 'Tell the pedlar to go on his way.'

Wu whispered to his father, and his father smiled. Yes, the pedlar could stop, for Wu wanted to buy something.

The pedlar spread out his wares in the gatehouse. Wu's father did not look at them; he had returned to his post by the gate. But Wu did not want his mother to see the pedlar's wares either. 'Please don't look,' he said to her. 'Please shut your eyes.'

His mother said she would shut her eyes, but she could not close her ears. 'I will go and talk to Su-Lan's mother for a while,' she told him.

'Come back by and by,' said Wu. He did not want her to look now, but it would be all right for her to come back after the pedlar had gone.

This time Wu hardly noticed the little toys made of wood. He was looking for something to buy for his mother and his father and Su-lan's mother. He finally picked out two fans and a pair of spectacles. Yes, he had enough money for those – just enough.

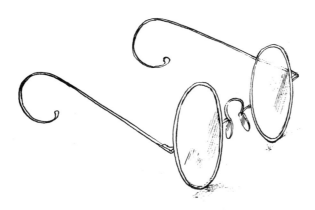

The fans were not the round kind; they were the kind that opened and closed. They were for his mother and Su-lan's mother. The spectacles were for his father. Wu admired these very much. The frames were made of tortoiseshell, and the glasses were blue.

When Wu had spent all his money, he suddenly thought of Su-lan. Surely he must give Su-lan a present, too! What could he do? He could not part with the fans and the spectacles. 'I have spent all my money, and yet I need to buy one thing more,' he said.

The pedlar thought for a moment. New Year's Day was coming, and that was a day when all children should be happy. 'Choose one thing more,' he said to Wu. 'You need not pay me for it. Just be sure it is a little thing and not very costly.'

Wu thanked the pedlar. He knew just what to choose: a little pink and green basket! 'I would like that,' he said.

'It is yours,' said the pedlar.

No, it was Su-lan's. Wu hoped that the little basket would make her happy on New Year's Day . . .

Wu's four brothers came home on New Year's Day, bringing many packages of bright red firecrackers. Su-lan set off a little string of small ones that sounded like crackling wood in a stove, and Wu set off three big ones that sounded like guns. Nobody felt sorry to see the Old Year go, for the New Year was bright and gay and noisy.

Wu was very happy, because Su-lan liked her basket, his father liked his spectacles, and his mother liked her fan. He was glad that he was big enough to work and earn money. He was one year older since the New Year had come.

The cakes the cook had made had writing on them. They said *Happy New Year*. And it was a happy New Year. There were good things to eat, and there were toys for the children. Even the pets were not forgotten. Ding received a new collar, and the cat received a little clay mouse . . .

'I wish New Year's Day would never end,' said Su-lan, swinging her green and pink basket to and fro.

'I wish that too,' said Wu. But night was coming, and soon it would be time to light the lanterns in the garden. Soon his brothers would set off the fireworks they had brought.

The four brothers had journeyed home from far away – two

from the city and one from the sea coast. The one who travelled with a camel train had come across the plains, and it was he who told Wu how big the world was. 'You can never reach the end of it, no matter how far you go,' he said. 'But when you are a traveller you see a large part of the world.'

'I have been across the river,' said Wu. He had seen a small part of the world. But the place he liked best of all was his own home.

Wu had made up his mind. When he was grown up he would not be a merchant, and he would not be a fisherman. He wanted to be a gatekeeper like his father, for exciting things happen when you live in a gatehouse.

He looked forward to all the days of this happy New Year. Spring would come, and the goldfish would be in the pond once more. Wu would watch the gate with his watchdog, Ding, who would look very fine in his bright new collar.

from *The Gatekeeper's Son*

# JANUARY 5th AND 6th

## Twelfth Night and Day

On the twelfth day after the birth of Jesus, so we are told, the Three Kings, led by a star, came to Bethlehem, bringing to the baby Jesus gifts of gold, frankincense and myrrh. And so throughout the Christian world Twelfth Day became a popular festival, originally held in honour of the Three Kings.

On Twelfth Night it was the custom to give a party. For the party a big cake was baked, and a bean and a pea were mixed with the dough. The cake was cut in slices, and handed round among the guests. The one who found the bean in his or her slice, was hailed as King; the one who found the pea was hailed as Queen. Paper crowns were put on their heads, and until midnight they ruled supreme over all the games and jollities.

> Now, now the mirth comes
> With the cake full of plums,
> Where Beane's the King of the sport here,
> Beside we must knowe
> The pea also
> Must revell as Queene for the night here.
>
> Which knowne, let us make
> Joy-sops with the cake,
> And let not a man then be seen here,
> Who inurged will not drinke
> To the base from the brink
> A health to the King and the Queene here.

Next crowne the bowle full
With gentle lamb's wooll;[1]
And sugar, nutmeg and ginger,
With store of ale too;
And this you must doe
To make the wassaille a stinger.

Give then to the King,
And the Queene wassailing:
And though with ale ye be whet here;
Yet part ye from hence,
As free from offence,
As when ye innocent met here.

*Robert Herrick*

It is said that when Saint Joseph of Arimathea went to Glastonbury he planted his staff in the ground, and it immedi-

[1] Lamb's Wooll: spiced ale.

ately took root and grew into a thorn tree, and that this thorn blossomed not in spring or summer but on Twelfth Night. At any rate, whether planted by Saint Joseph or not, there is a thorn tree in Glastonbury that blooms on Twelfth Night; and cuttings taken from this thorn, when they have grown into trees, also blossom on Twelfth Night. 'Last night the slip of Holy Thorn grafted last spring in the vicarage lower garden blossomed in an intense frost,' wrote Francis Kilvert in his diary, on Twelfth Day, 1879.

'In Russia on January 6th, for the Blessing of the Waters, a religious procession went to the banks of the Moskva, and halted before a large hole that had been cut in the ice. A bishop celebrated mass in the open air. The choir sang. To the sound of all the bells, a cross was plunged into the cold black waters. In a temperature of minus twenty degrees, the crowd watched the ceremony from the bank. When the procession of priests, deacons, banners, crosses and ikons had left the spot to return solemnly to the church, there were always a few courageous young fellows who promptly undressed, ran naked to the hole and plunged into the icy waters. They came out red as boiled lobsters with haggard eyes, shivering limbs, and laughter on their lips. Charitable spectators at once rushed towards them, rubbed them, wrapped them in coats, and gave them great draughts of vodka.'

*Henri Troyat*, Life in Russia under the last Tsar

# Not 'Zactly

## *Ruth Manning-Sanders*

The foolish boy stood with his back against the harbour wall and faced his tormentors. He didn't understand; no, he didn't

23

understand. A moment ago he had been alone with the big winter clouds and the wind and the sea-gulls. The wind had blown through the sleeves of his little jacket and changed his arms into wings, and he had flown up with the sea-gulls. He and hundreds of gulls together had wheeled screaming above the masts of the boats, up into the windy sky, round and round, *down*. 'Ai-ou! Ai-ou! Ha! ha! ha! Do you smell the fish, brother, boats full of fish, do you smell the good smell, brother? Ai-ou! Ai-ou! Ha! ha! ha!' Arms flapping, mouth open, screaming with joy, a sea-gull among sea-gulls – a moment ago.

But now everything had changed. He was shivering with misery; he was small and alone, with his back against the wall, and a gang of boys pranced round him, shouting and jeering, flapping their arms, not in joy but in mockery, mimicking his sea-gull cries. 'Foolish boy, foolish boy! Ai-ou, Ha! ha! ha! Foolish boy! Ai-ou!'

Their red faces, open grinning mouths, waving fists and trampling boots closed in upon him. One tweaked the cap off his head, another leaped on his toes, another swung a dead dog-fish – thump – across his chest. The foolish boy gasped and clutched the rough granite with his cold fingers. He felt sick, the bobbing faces and jumping bodies merged into an indistinct nightmare haze that filled the whole world; there were no gulls, no wind, no magnificent wintry clouds drifting across the sunlit sky, nothing but nightmare shapes and mockery . . .

There *was* something else. There was Fanny. Unseen by the foolish boy or his tormentors, she was pounding along the quay, her brown eyes scowling, her cheeks red with anger, her yellow hair blowing in the wind, her short green skirt flying up from her sturdy knees; one garter had snapped, one stocking was down from the energy of her running. A youthful, panting maenad, she whirled into the group of mockers. *Smack* went her right fist – and a nose spouted blood; *bang*

24

went her left arm – and a boy reeled. Shouting imprecations, hitting out like a boxer, she charged the whole gang of them, and as they scattered with cowardly catcalls, she pounced upon the foolish boy, shook him, and led him towards home.

Fanny was twelve, a strapping girl, not particularly intelligent, perhaps, but bursting with health and sisterly devotion. The foolish boy was nine, small, thin, and, according to Fanny, 'Not 'zactly'. Which meant that he was not just like other boys, because their dad had been drowned before he was born, and their mam had died in giving birth to him. They lived with Gran, and Fanny did the mothering. Practical, sturdy, and solid as a rock, she planted herself squarely between her foolish little brother and the cruelties of the world. But she couldn't be 'everywheres to wunst', and sometimes, when her back was turned, he would wander off by himself, and then there would be trouble, as now.

'Are you hurted? Why didn't you stay home? You're a naughty boy! You brought it on yourself, I'll skin 'em alive. I will! See, now m'hand's bleeding! No it ain't, that's Tommy Wattle's blood – the great beast!' Fanny let go of the foolish boy's shoulder to wipe her blood-stained fist on her stocking. 'Oh, my golly, now I've lost my garter, all through you!' She stared at the foolish boy. 'Where's your cap?'

'They threw it away.'

'They did? I'll learn 'em. I'll fetch policeman to 'em. Where to did they throw it?'

'I don't know.'

'You don't know nothing.'

The foolish boy endured her rating meekly; he understood that he was a great worry to her. Moreover he understood that she wasn't really angry with him. Moreover, the seagulls were again wheeling and screaming under the big white clouds, and there was a radiance at the back of his mind.

'I was flying,' he said.

'Oh, you was?' Fanny was looking about for his cap. She

25

spied it in a muddy shallow under the quay and clambered down an iron ladder to retrieve it. It was in 'some shape' she declared, when she had clambered up again. 'And boys can't fly,' she reminded him with severity.

The foolish boy said nothing. He could fly all right. He could do lots of things that Fanny said he couldn't do. But it was the things he could do, more than the things he couldn't do, that brought trouble upon him.

The 'shape' of his cap was now Fanny's theme. 'I don't know as I'll take you tonight, after all,' she threatened.

Tonight being Twelfth Night, the children of the village were going 'Guise Dancing': a name that held a memory of by-gone days, when the whole village was alight with mirth and pageantry in honour of Old Christmas. Then it was the grown-ups who, in the guise of strolling players, went from

house to house to give spirited performances of such old Cornish Drolls as *Duffy and the Devil* and *St George and the Turkish Knight*. But now the old plays were forgotten, and the entire affair was left to the children who, dressed up in anything that came to hand, formed themselves into groups and wandered about ringing at likely doorbells. If admitted, they would recite or sing a song, and receive largesse of pennies and cake.

'No,' said Fanny, as she wrung water out of the muddy cap. 'You've made enough trouble for one day. You best stay home with Gran.'

At this pronouncement the foolish boy's feet wanted to stop walking. But Fanny took his arm and hurried him along. The arm quivered under her resolute grip. She looked down and saw tears slowly trickling over the foolish boy's nose.

'What now?' she asked.

'The – the lantern,' whispered the foolish boy.

Fanny and her pals were going to carry lanterns made out of hollowed turnips; lanterns with round eyes and flaming mouths and cheeks that glowed golden from within. The foolish boy had seen them last night, lit up in a row on the kitchen dresser when Gran turned out the gas. The kitchen had been full of children jumping and shouting and clapping their hands, and the foolish boy had uttered a soft little cry and gone to bury his head in Gran's lap, because the joy of those lanterns had been almost more than he could bear.

'See, there's one for Osbert, too,' Gran had said. Osbert was the foolish boy's real name, but no one called him by it except Gran. 'He'll walk with the rest – oh yes he will – and his lantern will light up the darkness.'

But now it seemed he was to stay at home.

'Stop it, do,' said Fanny, as the tears rolled down his nose. 'You can take your lantern up to bed with you.'

No, oh no, no. That was not what the foolish boy wanted.

'I *would* take you,' explained Fanny. 'But I'm feared you'll shame me in one house or another.'

The foolish boy didn't answer. He stooped his head to wipe his eyes on his sleeve, and a tear fell on Fanny's hand.

'Well then – if I do take you – will you promise not to open your mouth?'

The foolish boy nodded.

'Nor throw yourself about, nor do nothing soft?'

The foolish boy nodded.

'Just stay close to me and keep quiet, see?'

The foolish boy nodded and nodded. He wouldn't open his mouth from that moment.

'All right,' said Fanny . . .

That night seven grotesque figures assembled in the court outside Gran's house. Four of them were girls and three were boys. The boys had black faces; one wore a long muslin frock with a pair of grey stays laced outside it, one capered in his

28

father's nightshirt, the third wore a piratical hat of red and black paper, a cardboard sword and a brown hearth rug draped over his trousers. The girls had paper flowers in their hair and old skirts of their mothers pinned round their slender hips. One had a parasol, one a mangy fur boa, and a patchwork quilt trailing from her shoulders to her heels, one a black lace shawl with a rent in it.

'Fanny! Fanny Corin!' They banged on Gran's door.

Fanny, arrayed in an ancient striped dress of Gran's, complete with bones and bustle, was tying the strings of a black sateen mask round the foolish boy's head. 'Don't you go for to soot up the precious lamb's face, now,' Gran had said, and she had cut a mask for him out of an old petticoat.

Through the holes in the mask the foolish boy's eyes stared at the table, where nine turnip lanterns burned palely orange under the white incandescent gaslight. 'On fire! People's heads on fire!' he thought, but he pressed his lips together and said nothing.

'Must guise you up a bit more'n that,' said Fanny, looking round the kitchen. She snatched up an antimacassar. 'This here'll do.'

'Fanny! Fanny Corin!'

'Coming!' Having looped the antimacassar round the foolish boy's waist, Fanny decked her own yellow head in Gran's wedding bonnet. The bonnet had a white ostrich feather and velvet ribbons to tie under the chin. She opened the door and the children crowded in.

Gran whipped off the foolish boy's antimacassar and dressed him properly in a thick scarf. 'He's only a looker-on,' she said. She didn't approve of her precious lamb being made to look foolish – perhaps he was foolish enough already. 'Now pick up your lanterns and away to go.'

Outside the stars were brilliant. The children walked single file through the narrow, crowded alleys by the water-front and up the hill where, among leafless trees and silent gardens,

29

stood the houses of the rich and great. The foolish boy walked last, keeping close to Fanny; eight fiery turnip heads marched in front of him, another fiery head swung from his careful hand. The dark sky glittered with endless jewels. The foolish boy thought he must be in heaven. The other children chattered and shouted, whistled and sang, but the foolish boy remembered his promise and pressed his lips together.

The chattering and shouting turned to anxious whispering outside the first house of call. The whispering turned to embarrassed giggling when the children were ushered into a lighted room where two ladies and two gentlemen were seated at a table playing cards. They were asked what they could do, and for a few moments nobody could do anything. Then Fanny stepped forward and breathlessly began a Sunday School poem entitled *I must not Tease my Mother*. The foolish boy hid behind a chair, the other children went on giggling. Fanny broke down in the third verse, and the ladies clapped and the gentlemen said bravo! Then they all four laughed and the children laughed also and, feeling more at their ease, sang *The First Noel* and *My Bonnie is over the Ocean*.

'That's not so bad, and thank you very much,' said one of the ladies. Then they were given sixpence, and told they might go.

So to the next house and the next. At one house they got a shilling and some nuts, at another threepence and slices of Christmas cake; at another the door was slammed in their faces by an irritable housemaid, at another they were encouraged to tell their names and ages. They gained in confidence as the evening wore on; Fanny was able to say *I must not Tease my Mother* right through without stumbling, the boy in the muslin dress remembered a comic song, two of the girls sang *The Keys of Heaven* very sweetly. They forgot to giggle and answered brightly when spoken to, all except the foolish boy who, mindful of his promise, pressed close to Fanny and shut his lips together.

*A sea-gull among sea-gulls*

'You see, he's not 'zactly,' explained Fanny, as she answered for him.

Out into the darkness, marching boldly up a path between tree branches on which the stars seemed to cluster like golden fruit. 'And this here house must be the last,' said Fanny as she reached for the door knocker. 'I promised our Gran us wouldn't be late.'

In this house there was a gentleman with a brown beard and green corduroy trousers, and a lady with gleaming hair and red corduroy trousers. There was also a black dog in a basket, and a white cat curled up on the hearth rug.

'Hullo?' said the lady.

'If you please, we're the Guise Dancers,' said Fanny.

'Go ahead,' said the gentleman, lounging with his hands in his pockets and his shoulders against the mantelpiece.

'I must not tease my mother,' began Fanny.

The lady looked at the gentleman, she pressed her lips together as if she, too, had promised not to say a word. The gentleman drew in his breath and groaned. His expression was that of a man suffering from severe toothache. The pain must have been very bad, for he writhed and screwed up his face.

'I must not tease my —' Fanny set off on another monotonous verse.

'Oh no, *no*!' interrupted the gentleman. 'That will *not* do!'

Fanny gaped at him open-mouthed. 'It's poytry, sir.'

'I *know*,' said the gentleman in exasperation. '*But* – Now listen to me children. I'll tell you a story about a wench called Duffy and a little imp called – Sit down, sit down on the floor, all of you. Comfortable? Right! Well then – Once upon a time . . .'

He told them a story which was the local version of *Rumpelstiltsken*. But it was far more exciting than *Rumpelstiltsken*; for there were witches in it, who rode through the air on stalks of ragwort and on three-legged stools, and they gathered in a

32

cave underground where a fire burned with a blue flame. And in and out of the fire a little imp kept hopping and skipping, and as he skipped he sang:

'Duffy, my lady, you'll never know – what?
That my name is Terrytop, Terrytop – top!'

All through the telling of this tale the foolish boy kept his eyes on the gentleman's face. He forgot that he was supposed to be disguised and pushed back the black mask that he might watch the better. But he wasn't seeing the gentleman. He was seeing the lazy Duffy crying in the garret because she couldn't spin the wool into yarn for the squire's stockings. He was seeing the little imp coming up through the garret floor, he was watching that imp as he set the black fleeces whirling round his head till they fell to the ground changed into heaps of glistening white yarn. He was seeing the witches flying through the air on their ragwort stalks and three-legged stools, he was seeing the little imp skipping through the blue flames and singing, 'Terrytop – top!'

The foolish boy became so excited that he forgot his promise and opened his mouth. 'Terrytop! Terrytop-top!' he shrilled.

Fanny gave him a nudge that made him shut his lips again. The gentleman smiled at him and finished the story.

'Now,' he said, 'if you're real Guise Dancers get up and act that story. For that's what they did in the old days!'

The children stood up and looked at one another. They felt silly. 'Us don't know how,' giggled Fanny.

'Try,' said the gentleman. 'You' (to Fanny) 'shall be Duffy. And you' (to the boy with the piratical hat) 'shall be the squire. And you' (to the girl with the fur boa) 'shall be Duffy's mother. The rest can be witches. And this little fellow here will be Terrytop – eh, sonny?'

The foolish boy nodded, and his eyes shone.

'Oh no, sir,' said Fanny, 'he belongs to keep his mouth shut.'

33

'Why's that?'

'Well, you see, sir, he's not 'zactly.'

'Rubbish!' exclaimed the gentleman.

The foolish boy was so excited that his feet refused to keep still, and his mouth refused to keep shut. He began skipping about the room and piping:

'Duffy, my lady, you'll never know – what?
That my name is Terrytop, Terrytop – top!'

For the foolish boy's eyes the room disappeared. There was the black cave with water dripping from the roof. There was the fire with the blue flames. There were the witches. The water dripped into the fire and hissed. The foolish boy skipped in and out of the blue flames.

'I call that really brilliant, don't you?' said a voice from somewhere within the cave. 'Now, let's begin from the beginning. Come on, Duffy's mother, take off that fur arrangement of yours, and beat your lazy daughter with it.'

It was a grand game, and once they had fairly started on it the children forgot their silly feeling and played their parts with gusto. But as to the foolish boy, it was no game to him; it was life, life! Like a dog on a leash he shivered and strained till his turn came. And when it came – 'Would you believe it?' thought Fanny. 'If he ain't some clever, after all!'

The play came to an end. The children were given sixpence a piece, and told they had done very well. But the foolish boy was shaken by both hands at once, and told he had done excellently. 'When I want a young actor for a play I mean to write,' said the gentleman, 'I shall know where to find him. And now Fanny, my dear – that's your name isn't it? Yes, well Fanny, I want you to promise me something.'

'Yes, sir?'

'Promise me,' said the gentleman solemnly, 'that you will never, never again tell any one that your brother is not 'zactly. Say he's different, if you like. Some people *are* different,

34

thank heaven! And, by the way – listen to me a minute, all of you. What do you mean by not 'zactly? You mean different, don't you? But there's a good difference as well as a bad one, there's a – (he turned to the lady) "a superlative difference". So promise, Fanny.'

Feeling curiously abashed, Fanny promised.

'Then goodnight to you all,' said the gentleman, flinging open the front door.

'Goodnight,' said the lady.

'Goodnight,' called the children from the doorstep.

The turnip lanterns were burned out and forgotten, but the stars were still glittering in the dark sky. The foolish boy looked up at the stars, and every one of them seemed to be glittering inside his own head. 'Hurr-a-ah!' he called shrilly and began to run down the hill.

'Hurr-a-ah!' cried the other children pelting after him.

Hurrah! Hurrah! Hurrah! The stars danced among the bare tree branches, the road echoed to the running feet, the night rang with jubilant cries. 'Hurrah! Hurrah!' Fanny pounding along like a young carthorse, with Gran's wedding bonnet dangling from her neck, and Gran's bustle jigging at her back, began to laugh and shout. 'Clever as clever, clever'n all of us, hurray for our foolish boy!'

Her heart was glowing with sisterly pride. She gave such an energetic leap towards the stars that the frail skirt of Gran's old striped gown split with a rending sound across her knees. But she only laughed the louder. There was her little clever brother running ahead of them all – her little *different* brother! 'And just let me catch any one saying he's not 'zactly,' thought Fanny. 'Just let me catch 'em!'

*Ruth Manning-Sanders*

February

# FEBRUARY 1st

## Saint Bride's Day

She is the patron saint of milkmaids. In England we call her Saint Bride, but in Ireland, where she was born, and also in the Isle of Man, she is always known as Saint Bridget.

Bridget was not quite like other little girls; the birds knew that. When she called them, they would come to perch on her hand. Then she would stroke their heads with one finger, and laugh and talk to them; and when she told them to fly away again, they circled about her, singing for joy.

Once her mother sent her milking with the maids for butter-making. But Bridget gave away all the milk in her pails to the poor. What her mother thought about that, we are not told; but after the maids had brought in their milk, and the butter-making began, Bridget prayed, the butter doubled itself, and the extra butter young Bridget also gave away to the poor. So you can understand why she is considered to be the patron saint of milkmaids.

As soon as she was old enough, Bridget became a nun – the first nun in Ireland – and built for herself a little cell under an oak tree. Her cell was called *Kil-dara* (the cell of the oak.) By and by other nuns came to join her, the lonely little cell developed into a great nunnery, and round the nunnery arose the city of Kildare.

# A Milking Song

## *Fiona Macleod*

O sweet Saint Bride of the
Yellow, yellow hair;
Paul said, and Peter said,
And all the saints alive or dead
Vowed she had the sweetest head,
Bonnie, sweet Saint Bride of the
Yellow, yellow hair.

White may my milking be,
White as thee:
Thy face is white, thy neck is white,
Thy hands are white, thy feet are white,
For thy sweet soul is shining bright.
O dear to me,
O dear to see
Saint Bridget white!

Safe thy way is, safe, O
Safe, Saint Bride:
May my kye come home at even,
None be fallin', none be leavin',
Dusky even, breath-sweet even,
Here, as there, where O
Saint Bride thou

Keepest tryst with God in heav'n,
Seest the angels bow
And souls be shriven –
Here as there, 'tis breath-sweet even
Far and wide –

Singeth thy little maid
Safe in thy shade
Bridget, Bride!

*Fiona Macleod*

# A Japanese Snow Festival

If you wish to see a snow man thirty-three feet high, you must
go in February to Sapphora, the capital of the Japanese island,
Hokkaido. Yes, there he squats, built by soldiers out of two

hundred and twenty truckloads of snow, an image of the great Myo-o, the Buddhist god of love. Ah, but he is a ferocious fellow, this god of love, with his fierce eyes, broad, flat nose, wide open mouth with its rows of glittering teeth, and its two tusks sticking out from the corners of his lower lip! In his six hands he clutches various symbols of his majesty: a lightning bolt, a bell, a bow and arrow, a lotus – and he lives for exactly three days, to be afterwards hacked to pieces by the same soldiers who created him.

But during those three days over six million people will have gathered to gaze fascinated at his awesome presence. For this is the Japanese Snow Festival; nor is the great god Myo-o alone in his glory. Other giants surround him: there are huge frozen dinosaurs, there are snow demons with glittering eyes,

there are fabulous monsters, there is even an ice railway engine, there is an enormous ape, King Kong, there are vast snow towers and buildings to represent the town itself, and there are snow figures of the workmen who built the town.

Impermanent as the snow flakes out of which they are made, all these wonderful images are doomed, after their three days glory, to be levelled with the ground. But they will rise again in their glory when next year's winter shall have brought the snow again; and with the snow an ever increasing crowd of fur-muffled visitors to gaze in delighted wonderment at this unique spectacle.

# Of The Great Festival Which The Khan Holds On New Year's Day

## *Marco Polo*

The beginning of their New Year is in the month of February, and on that occasion the Great Khan and all his subjects make such a feast as I now describe.

It is the custom that on this occasion the Khan and all his subjects should be clothed entirely in white; so, that day, everybody is in white, men and women, great and small. And this is done in order that they may thrive all through the year, for they deem that white clothing is lucky. On that day also all the people of all the provinces and governments and kingdoms and countries that owe their allegiance to the Khan bring him great presents of gold and silver, and pearls and gems, and rich textures of divers kinds. And this they do that the Emperor throughout the year may have abundance of treasure and enjoyment without care. And the people also

42

make presents to each other of white things, and embrace and kiss and make merry, and wish each other happiness and good luck for the coming year. On that day, I can assure you, among the customary presents there shall be offered to the Khan from various quarters more than 100,000 white horses, beautiful animals and richly caparisoned.

On that day, also, the Khan's elephants, amounting fully to 5000 in number, are exhibited, all covered with rich and gay housings of inlaid cloth representing beasts and birds, and each of them carries on his back two splendid coffers; all of these being filled with the Emperor's plate and other costly furniture required for the court on the occasion of the White Feast. And these are followed by a vast number of camels which are laden with things needful for the Feast. All these are paraded before the Emperor, and it makes the finest sight in the world.

# FEBRUARY 14th

## Saint Valentine's Day

Valentine, the lovers' saint, was a Roman priest who suffered martyrdom in the third century.

But you must know that long before this, in ancient Roman times, a merry festival, called Lupercalia, was held during February in honour of the great god Pan. And, amongst other ceremonies, the names of various willing young women were put into a box, and shaken up. Then, if a lad wanted a companion for the festival, he drew a name out of the box, and the one whose name he drew became his 'girl' for the time being. So popular was this custom that it spread right through Europe and into Britain. But when the people became Christians the priests disapproved of such flippant doings. So what did they do? They changed the feast of Lupercalia into the feast of Saint Valentine, and instead of girls' names they had the names of various saints put into a box for people to draw out. And to the saint you drew, prayers would be offered.

Naturally, nobody thought much of *that* idea! And naturally the lads still hankered after their girl friends. So they went on with their own private amusement.

Besides drawing lots, there were other ways of happening upon your Valentine. Often it was the first person of the opposite sex you saw on Saint Valentine's morning. And the married folk, as well as the unmarried, had their Valentines, as we learn from the diary of Samuel Pepys:

'*February 14th, 1667:* This morning came to my wife's bedside (I being up dressing myself) little Will Mercer to be her Valentine and brought her name written upon blue paper in gold letters, done by himself, very prettily, and we both well pleased with it.'

'*February 14th, 1661:* Up early and to Sir W. Batten's . . . and took Mrs Martha for my Valentine (which I do only for complacency), and Sir W. Batten he go in the same manner to my wife, and so we were very merry,'

(Your Valentine expected to be given a present):

'*February 22nd, 1661:* My wife to Sir W. Batten's, and there sat a while; he having yesterday sent my wife half-a-dozen pair of gloves and a pair of silk stockings and garters for her Valentine.'

'*February 22nd, 1661:* In the afternoon my wife and I and Mrs Martha Batten, my Valentine, to the Exchange, and there upon a pair of embroidered and six pair of plain white gloves, I laid out 40 shillings upon her.'

But to have chosen someone as your Valentine did not necessarily imply any lasting attachment:

'*February 14th, 1662:* (Valentine's Day) I did this day purposely shun to be seen at Sir W. Batten's, because I would not have his

44

daughter' (Mrs Martha) 'to be my Valentine, as she was the last year, there being no great friendship between us now.'

And before we leave Saint Valentine, there is one thing more to be said. This is the day on which the birds are supposed to choose their mates:

> Hail, Bishop Valentine! whose day this is:
> All the air is thy diocese,
> And all the chirping choristers
> And other birds are thy parishioners:
> Thou marryest every year
> The lyric lark and the grave whispering dove;
> The sparrow that neglects his life for love,
> The household bird with the red stomacher;
> Thou mak'st the blackbird speed as soon
> As doth the goldfinch or the halcyon –
> This day more cheerfully than ever shine,
> This day which might inflame thyself, old Valentine!
>
> *John Donne*

March

# MARCH 17th

## Saint Patrick's Day

Patrick, who lived in the 4th century, is the patron saint of
Ireland. He came of a noble Scottish family; but when he was
sixteen he was captured by pirates, and sold into slavery in
Ireland, where his master employed him as a swineherd. He

served this master for seven years; but at last, with the help of some friendly sailors, he escaped and, after many adventures, reached Italy. Eventually he was made a bishop and sent back to Ireland to convert the heathen.

In those days the High King of Tara ruled supreme over all the kings of Ireland. And by the High King's orders, every fire in Ireland must be put out at Easter and relighted from a fire in the King's own castle on the Hill of Tara. The penalty for disobeying this order was death. But one Easter the High King looked from the Hill of Tara, and what did he see? A great fire blazing away defiantly on an opposite hill. Who dared to have lighted it, and what did it mean? The furious King sent his soldiers hurrying to the hill, where they found Saint Patrick, all alone, piling wood onto the fire he had kindled. The soldiers brought Patrick to the King. The King was raging; but Patrick explained that he had made the fire as a sign that Christ, risen from the dead on Easter morning, was the Light of the World. And the King, admiring the saint's courage, forgave him. Indeed, some say that the King was then and there converted to Christianity. But others say not.

## The Rune of Saint Patrick

At Tara in this fateful hour
I place all Heaven with its power,
And the sun with its brightness,
And the snow with its whiteness,
And fire with all the strength it hath,
And lightning with its rapid wrath,
And the winds with their swiftness along their path,
And the sea with its deepness,
And the rocks with their steepness,

And the earth with its starkness:
All these I place,
By God's almighty help and grace,
Between myself and the powers of darkness.

from *The Book of Hymns*, translated from the Gaelic by Charles Mangan.

The shamrock, a small clover-like plant, which bears three leaves on each stem, is said to have been used by Saint Patrick as an illustration of the Trinity. So, in honour of the saint, if you live where shamrocks grow, you wear one in your hat on March 17th. In America people wear little artificial shamrocks; and also it is proper to put on something green, and to have corned beef and cabbage for dinner.

# Shrove Tuesday

Shrove Tuesday is the last day before Lent. And as in Lent it has been (and still is with many people) the custom to fast and think seriously of your faults and try to amend them, on Shrove Tuesday you make merry and have a good tuck in – especially of pancakes.

Here is a description of the pre-Lenten Carnival in Nice in the south of France:

'The great day of the festival is usually on what is called in Great Britain Shrove Tuesday or Pancake Day. In France it is known as Mardi Gras, or Fat Tuesday.

At the Carnival season the streets are gaily decorated with flags and festoons of flowers, and at night are lit up with thousands of coloured lamps. Most of the shops close, and

51

*There is even an ice railway engine*

everybody turns out to have a good time. Crowds go about the streets in fancy costumes, wearing masks or false noses and wigs, and very funny they look. Many carry bladders tied on sticks, with which they belabour each other, pelting passers-by with flowers or confetti, as at weddings in England.

Everywhere there are pierrots, clowns, Red Indians, men in armour, columbines, bears, monkeys, giants and dwarfs, and both day and night the streets are filled with revellers dancing, singing, blowing tin trumpets, and generally behaving like a lot of children, which indeed they are. Everybody is good-natured and prepared to take all that happens in good part.

On certain days battles of flowers and confetti are held. Gaily decorated, flower-decked carriages and triumphal cars pass in procession. On some are drawn huge grotesque figures made of basket work . . . The festivals usually begin with the entry of King Carnival, a gigantic figure mounted on a car. Later this figure is burnt, with a grand display of fireworks and perhaps a torchlight procession.

All sorts of sports – racing, shooting, regattas and masked balls are held, and the fun goes on almost continually for about a week. The children are not forgotten – they have their own special fancy-dress balls and battles of flowers and sweetmeats.'

from *The Wonder Book of Children of all Nations*
(Ed. Harry Golding)

# Mardi Gras in New England, 1850

## *Sir Charles Lyall*

It was the last day of Carnival . . . There was a grand procession parading the streets, almost every one dressed in the most

52

grotesque attire, troops of them on horseback, some in open carriages, with bands of music, and a variety of costumes . . . some as Indians, with feathers in their heads, and one jolly little man as Mardi Gras himself. All wore masks, and here and there in the crowd, or stationed in a balcony above, we saw persons armed with bags of flour, which they showered down copiously on any one who seemed particularly proud of his attire . . . We were amused by observing the ludicrous surprise, mixed with contempt, of several unmasked, still, grave Anglo-Americans from the North, who were witnessing, for the first time, what seemed to them so much mummery and tomfoolery.

from *A Second Visit to the United States 1850*


# Pancake Day at Great Pagwell

## *Norman Hunter*

*Professor Branestawm invites his friends – the Vicar, the Mayor, the Assistant Mayor, the Librarian, and Colonel Dedshott to Tea and Pancakes at 4·30 on Shrove Tuesday.*

*His housekeeper, Mrs Flittersnoop, has also invited the four firemen, because she rather liked one of the dark, curly-haired ones, and couldn't very well ask him without the others.*

*When they have all arrived, the Professor makes a little speech:*

'Ladies and Gentlemen, I have asked you all here to-day to show you an invention I have invented. It is something that has never been done before. It will be welcomed throughout the world as the greatest er um invention since the – er um – since the – er – er – '

'Bravo!' cried Colonel Dedshott, beginning to applaud like anything, but stopping rather suddenly when he found nobody else was doing it.

53

'I have – er – er –' went on the Professor, 'that is to say, never before – er um – for the first time in history of ah – um – er I will show you my invention and you may judge for yourself.'

He stepped across to the folding doors that closed off the dining-room from what was supposed to be the drawing-room, but was really the Professor's study. He flung open the doors, one of which caught the Mayor's chair and whisked it away, letting the Mayor down bump this time, so the Vicar helped him up.

There was nothing in the Professor's study except the fearful muddle of nearly everything that was always there, if you can call that nothing, which of course you can't really, but you see what it was. The new invention wasn't there.

'Oh, I remember now,' said the Professor, unfastening the safety-pins that kept his coat together in place of the buttons he couldn't remember to have sewn on, and looking at a piece of paper he had taken from his waistcoat pocket. 'I left it in the kitchen. Wait a minute, don't go away, I'll go and get it.'

And off he went, while the others looked at each other, and wondered when the pancakes were coming, and tried to think of chatty things to say, but couldn't think of any . . .

Colonel Dedshott screwed his eyeglass into his eye and dropped it out again seven times, then he was just getting himself ready to say 'Bravo' again, and applaud a bit to get things going as it were, when there was a most unmentionable bumping and rattling outside the door, and presently the Professor began to come in very slowly and difficultly because he was all surrounded and tangled up with a sort of machine of some kind.

It was the great invention.

'My guess is that it is a cinematograph,' said the Vicar, thinking he might be a bit jolly.

'I think it's a fire escape,' piped up the dark curly-haired fireman, and Mrs Flittersnoop said 'Bravo' very softly to herself.

54

By this time the Professor had got himself untangled from the machine.

'Behold', he said, 'my greatest and latest invention, the Pancake-Making Machine.'

'Bravo!' roared Colonel Dedshott . . .

'This is Pancake Day,' went on the Professor, taking his four pairs of spectacles off, and getting them just as mixed up as he usually got his five pairs. 'It is a festival that is inclined to die out, because although people like pancakes they won't trouble to cook them. Too much trouble. Too much mess. That is what people say.'

At this Mrs Flittersnoop said 'Bravo!' out loud because she was one of the people who had said that to the Professor.

'With this machine,' said the Professor, 'pancakes are as easy as pie to make.'

'Begging your pardon, I'm sure,' put in Mrs Flittersnoop, 'but pie isn't easy to make sir, that it isn't, not unless you've got a light hand with the paste, not but what my pies aren't always what they should be and no great trouble either, sir, but you know what folks is – are,' she finished.

'Er-er-yes,' said the Professor. He put some of his pairs of spectacles on and crammed the rest in his pockets, where some of them fell through holes on to the floor. He was going to say a lot more about pancakes, but Mrs Flittersnoop had put it out of his head, so he thought he had better demonstrate the machine.

'Here,' he explained, pointing to different parts of the machine, 'are the flour bin, the egg receptacle, the milk churn, and the sugar castor and the lemon squisher . . .

'This is the pancake pan,' . . . 'and this is the thicknessing regulator, by means of which you can have pancakes any thickness you like . . .

'Here is the centrifugal tossing gear with adjustable self-changing height regulator, and my own patent device for calculating the number of tosses required for pancakes of

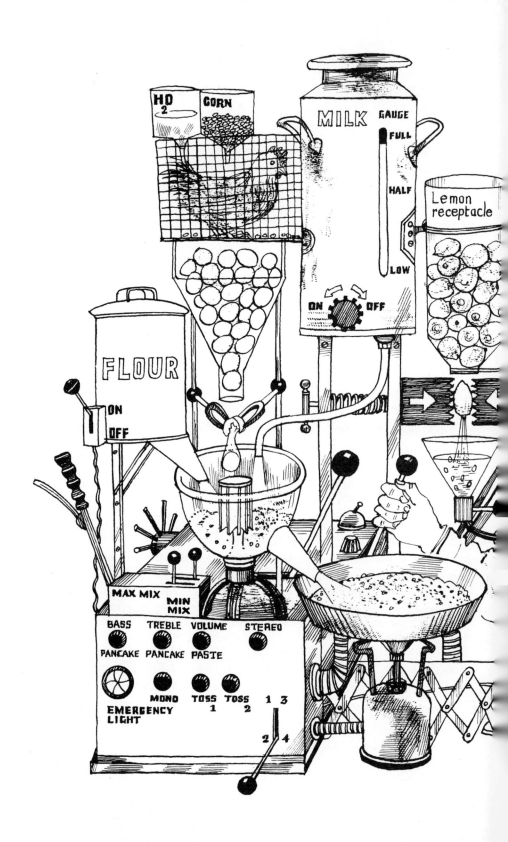

different thicknesses.'

'Will it go wrong?' asked the Library man, who had heard about the Professor's machines before.

'Certainly not,' said Colonel Dedshott very quickly, because the Professor's explanation was making his head go round as usual. As a matter of fact he knew the Professor's inventions a great deal better than the Library man and thought it definitely likely that this one would go wrong, but he was going to stick up for the Professor. His military training had made him awfully fierce and earnest about sticking up for people.

'Now,' said the Professor, 'for the pancakes.'

He pulled a lever, turned a handle, twiddled a knob, and pressed a button . . .

'Fiz, whirrr pop chug chug ps-s-s-s-s clang,' went the

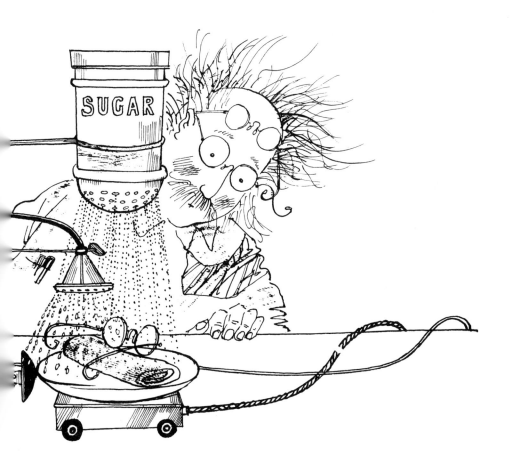

machine. Wheels went round. Splutterings occurred. There were floppy sounds and hissing noises. Then suddenly there was quite a loud pop, and a pancake shot up into the air, turned over exactly once, and dropped back into the machine.

'Bravo!' cried the Colonel, beginning to applaud again, but the Professor shushed him.

More fizzes and hisses and whirrings came from the machine. A plate which had been heating over a sort of gas-ring kind of arrangement which worked without gas, was slid forward, the pancake dropped daintily upon it, all rolled up and sugared, and wearing the Professor's fifth pair of spectacles, which he had dropped into the machine whilst inventing it.

'*Voila!*' said the Professor, handing it to the Mayor, who ate it all up, but left the spectacles like a fishbone on the side of his plate, while the eyes of the four firemen goggled so much that they nearly fell out on to the table.

'Bravo!' cried the Colonel again, rather faintly this time . . . because he was so empty inside himself.

The Professor manipulated the machine again, there were more fizzings, another pop, and soon another pancake, which was given to the Assistant Mayor, who ate it more quickly than the Mayor, because he hadn't had such a big dinner.

'I believe it will go wrong,' said the Library man, who hadn't got a pancake yet.

The next pancake went to the Vicar, and the next should have been for the Library man only the Mayor got it first. Then the four firemen began to clamour slightly because their turn seemed so long in coming round and they were used to having everything happening fearfully quickly. You know: 'ding-a-dong, fire, fire, boots on, helmets on, ding-a-dong, rush-a-rattle, ladders up, hose out, fire out, ding-a-dong, home again.'

The Professor turned the machine on a bit quicker and managed to get pancakes round to almost everyone, while the Mayor was able to stop three that were passed his way round.

'Now it *will* go wrong,' said the Library man.

58

'Bravo,' said the Colonel with his mouth full, his enthusiasm getting the better of his manners. 'Wonderful, marvellous, um yum, delightful, what!'

The four firemen finished their pancakes just five times as quickly as the Mayor took over his first one, which was exactly three and a half seconds less than it took them to get the fire engine out on a fine day, and passed their plates for more. The Mayor passed five plates, four for himself and one for the Assistant Mayor.

Professor Branestawm turned the machine on full speed. Pancakes came rolling out. The party was beginning to be most successful. Then all of a sudden there was a loud click and an extra whizzy whizz from inside the machine and the Professor came over all pale.

'Dear me!' he began, while Mrs Flittersnoop, who was half-way through a pancake, hurriedly hid under the table, expecting the worst, though she didn't know what it might be.

'Whiziziziz POP,' went the machine and a larger and thicker pancake than any shot out of the machine higher than it was supposed to, turned over eight-and-a-half times and dropped on the Professor's head, where it enveloped him like an unreasonable hat ten sizes too large.

'Wuff a g–g–g–g–gg, m–m–m–m–mm pwuff,' spluttered the Professor.

'Whizz, pop,' went the machine, and out shot another pancake which made straight for the Mayor, but missed him and stuck to the wall.

'I knew it would go –' began the Library man, leaning back in his chair, but a pancake landed on his mouth, so he said no more. His turn had come at last.

'Whizz pop whizz pop pop pop popperty pop pop,' faster and ever so much faster flew the pancakes. Thicker and thicker. Bigger and bigger. They came out flatways and edgeways. They shot high in the air and stuck to the ceiling. One sailed across the room and hit the Vicar in the waistcoat . . . Pop,

59

poppety, pop, pop, pop. It was like a machine-gun but much more sploshy.

The Professor struggled out of his pancake just in time for another one to drop over him. Two pancakes were on the clock, four were draped over the light. The Mayor was eating his way through a complete set of pancakes of varying sizes that had fallen in front of him. The four firemen put their helmets on and brandished their axes, but only succeeded in smashing two cups, one saucer, and the sugar basin. Mrs Flittersnoop put her head gingerly out from under the table and was immediately gummed to the carpet by a three-foot pancake two inches thick that had just shot out.

Quicker and quicker fell the pancakes. The pops began to get louder and the pancakes grew bigger. Pop bong bang boom! Roman candles weren't in it. Professor Branestawm was running round the room covered in pancakes and with spectacles sticking out all over him. The Library man got up to go, just managed to dodge an extra huge pancake, sat down exhausted on the pancake he had dodged, and couldn't move.

'Help!' roared the Colonel. 'The machine's gone wild! Stop it, Professor! By Jove, sir, the thing's mad. When I was in . . .' A five-foot pancake whistled past the Colonel's ear, shot through the window and suffocated four dozen assorted plants in the garden.

'Wah!' roared the Colonel his warlike spirit roused. Bong, bang, boom, thud, echoed the pancake artillery. The Colonel seized the poker and dashed valiantly at the machine, skewering nine enormous pancakes on his make-do sword as he ran.

Pop, boom, crash, wallop pop whizz bang rattle crash – oo-er bong, by Jove crash, thud. How the Colonel attacked the machine! How the pancakes thudded on the ceiling! How the poker crashed amongst the cog-wheels! Everyone got under the table to hide. It fell to pieces under the strain, but a ten-foot pancake flopped rather wearily over all of them, so they were hidden just the same.

60

Crash bang bong smack – 'When I was at' – flop crash bing. 'By Jove!' Splosh. 'What!'

At last the fight was over. The pancake machine wheezed and stopped. The poker was nearly tied in a knot, and the Colonel wore on his chest a very small thick pancake, which the machine with its last expiring pop had managed to plant there like a sort of medal.

from *The Incredible Adventures of Professor Branestawm*

# Easter Day

The celebration of Easter is far, far older than Christianity. For Easter is *Eostre*, the pagan goddess of the spring. And in pagan times all fires were extinguished in her honour, and relighted from a special sacred fire. (If you turn back to Saint Patrick's Day, you will see how the High King of Tara kept up this custom in pagan Ireland.) Well, the Christians took over this pagan custom; and in old times, in England, all the fires and lights in the church were extinguished, the ashes and embers taken out and replaced by fresh fires and candles. These were relit from a special enormous Paschal Candle. This huge candle was lit on Easter Eve in a pitch dark church, from a flint and steel. In Durham Cathedral the Paschal Candle, so we are told, reached almost to the roof, and had to be lit by a priest standing on a great ladder.

From the relit candles the parishioners took tapers to relight the fires on their own hearths, which had previously been cleaned and filled with flowers and branches.

In pagan times in England great bonfires were lit, in which a doll, representing winter, was burnt. Later on, in Christian times, a figure representing Judas was burnt, instead of the 'winter doll'.

Eggs are associated with Easter because the egg is a symbol of new life, and Easter is the time of life's resurrection; so eggs are a traditional fare for Easter Sunday. One of the popes, Pius V, in order to impress upon people the true meaning of the Easter egg, composed a special prayer for the use of the English:

'Bless, O Lord, we beseech Thee, this Thy creature of eggs, that it may become a wholesome sustenance to Thy faithful servants, eaten in thankfulness to Thee, on account of the Resurrection.'

## The Easter Hare

Long, long ago, there was a village where the people were very poor. One Easter time the mothers had no money to buy the presents of sweets they usually gave their children on Easter Sunday. They were very sad for they knew how disappointed the children would be.

'What shall we do?' they asked each other, as they drew water from the well.

'We have plenty of eggs,' sighed one.

'The children are tired of eggs,' said another.

Then one of the mothers had an idea, and before dinner-time all the mothers in the village knew about it, but not a single child.

Early on Easter morning, the mothers left their homes and went into the woods with little baskets on their arms. It was quite impossible to see what they had in the baskets as they were covered with coloured cloths. When the mothers returned home, the cloths were tied about their heads like head-squares, and the baskets were filled with wild flowers.

'My mother went to pick flowers for Easter this morning,'

said one child, as they all walked together to church.

'So did mine!' said another.

'And mine too!' said all the others, and laughed for they were happy and it was Easter Sunday.

When they came out of church, the children were told to go and play in the woods before dinner. Off they ran, laughing and talking. The girls picked flowers and the boys climbed trees, when someone shouted, 'Look what I've found!'

'A RED egg!'

'I've found a BLUE one!'

'Here's a nestful! All different colours!'

They ran about searching in the bushes and filling their pockets and hats.

'What kind of eggs are they?' they asked each other.

'They're too big for wild birds' eggs.'

'They're the same size as hens' eggs!'

'Hens don't lay eggs these bright colours, silly!'

Just then a hare ran out from behind a bush.

'They're hares' eggs!' cried the children. 'The hare laid the eggs! Hurrah for the Easter Hare!'

*A German Legend*

# Easter in Athens

## *Barbara Whelpton*

Anne had known Hermes and Julia Aspiotti when they had spent two months in England the previous year, but she had never seen the children.

On the train going to Athens, Hermes had told her about them. Helen, called Eleni in Greek, was eight years old. Her brother, Tino, would be six in the summer. The whole family

63

lived in a modern house at Psychico just outside Athens. They had a small garden and several balconies so that, in the hot weather, they could sleep outside.

They all spoke English very well.

As it was holiday time, Hermes said that the children would be waiting excitedly to see their new English friend. Indeed they were looking out for her at the front door, and fell over each other to greet her. They were so anxious to be friendly that they got Greek and English muddled up and Anne found it difficult to understand all the things that they tried to tell her about Easter.

Tino and Helen loved Easter. Holy Week in Greece is devoted by all Orthodox Christians to religious ceremonies. In the theatres and cinemas only religious films and plays are shown. The children had seen a film illustrating the Easter story and were anxiously awaiting Saturday night when they would stay up until midnight to see the great procession.

On Saturday morning Helen and Tino helped the two maids to dye eggs green and blue and red. Elizabeth, the cook, tied leaves round some of the eggs before putting them into the boiling dye so that a white pattern would be left.

There was plenty to be done all the morning. The Easter lamb had to be bought and got ready for roasting on Sunday. Presents and greetings had to be left at friends' homes, and the house decorated with spring flowers. Elizabeth was busy finishing off an elaborate centrepiece of chicken and eggs in coloured icing and chocolate which she had made for the table.

They all had a long rest in the afternoon as they were to be up very late. Agnes, the younger maid, had caught a cold and was running a temperature by the evening, so she could not go, as there was quite a cold north wind. She was terribly disappointed and begged the family to bring her home a lighted candle so that she could put it under the ikon above her bed.

The Aspiottis and Elizabeth and Anne went to a little church about a mile away, carrying white candles to be lighted later.

They arrived at a quarter to twelve, just as the lights and candles in the church were extinguished to symbolize the darkness of the grave. Only the oil lamp, which burns perpetually before the ikon of Christ on the high altar, was left glowing. They stood watching at the bottom of the church steps and could just see, through the gloom, the priest appear from behind the altar screen. He had a lighted candle in his hand, and walked to the door chanting 'Come ye and take light from the Eternal Light!' The congregation crowded round to light their candles from the sacred flame and to pass it on to each other.

A platform had been erected outside the church and decorated with flags and flowers and candles. The priest and acolytes and some of the choir mounted the platform to continue the service under the open sky, as it is believed that the heavens shower blessings on mankind when the resurrection is acclaimed. The priest went on to chant the story of the Marys at the sepulchre, and their astonishment that the stone had been rolled away, until he came to the angel's words, 'He is not here; he is risen: *Christos anesti* – Christ is risen.' Church bells rang out, a lighted emblem was held high above the heads of the congregation and the cry '*Alithos anesti* – He is risen indeed' was sung by everyone present. Fireworks were let off and greetings exchanged. Latecomers lighted their candles from those of the people already there.

The wind blew out a candle and immediately the owner went to relight it from another. '*Christos anesti*' he said, and the answer came '*Alithos anesti*'. Anne was to hear and give this greeting many a time during the next few hours and even to see it printed in bright colours on strips of cheap paper and pasted across the mirrors in a restaurant or stuck on the windows of a shop.

Many people were carrying hard-boiled eggs, for the egg is a symbol of life and happiness to the Greeks, but they believe that they must take the trouble to break the egg themselves in order to let these blessings escape. Couples were breaking each other's eggs, according to custom. To do this, one person holds his red-dyed egg firmly in the hand whilst the other brings the end of his egg sharply down upon it. People try to break as many eggs as they can before their own is broken.

All over Greece the church bells were ringing, people were rejoicing. The King and Queen were in Athens cathedral and had lighted a candle and exchanged the Easter greeting with the archbishop. From chapels and churches in every region worshippers were trailing home, lighted candles in their hands. Tiny specks of light were flickering everywhere. The sky was deep blue, cut across by the scarlet of a soaring rocket, or split up by the glitter of a falling fairy light. In monasteries built on the peaks of the mountains, priests were ringing the bells and celebrating Easter Day.

The Acropolis was floodlit and the Parthenon seemed to be sailing the sky like a magnificent ship. For more than two thousand years this temple, built by the ancient Greeks for the goddess Athena, had looked down to the city below and witnessed scenes like this. Perhaps the sacrifices of the early Greeks to their ancient gods had been more elaborate, their ceremonial costume more gorgeous, but Anne felt that they could not really have been more impressive than the magic of the thousands of lights travelling slowly down from the churches on the hills to homes in the valley below.

The Aspiottis started to walk home. The road was rough and badly lighted and Anne had difficulty in keeping her candle alight. Experienced Greeks held theirs cupped in their hands, protected from the wind. A few late buses passed, packed with homegoers carrying lighted candles. Two boys on donkeys ambled by, guiding their beasts with their feet and using both hands to protect the flame.

Hermes was determined to get an extra candle home alight for Agnes. She would be lying awake so that she could place it herself by her ikon. He went on in front, the others dragging

66

*And had to be lit by a priest
standing on a great ladder*

behind, keeping pace with the children who were very sleepy. They could see his flame wavering ahead of them, and it lighted their path. 'Nearly home,' he called out and then tripped on a stone, lost his balance and sat down in a ditch, his feet up in the air. He did not try to save himself but flung his arms above his head and managed to keep both candles from going out. The family had to help him to his feet as he had no hands free. He was not badly hurt and managed to limp home and present Agnes with her candle still burning. She lighted the lamp under her ikon from it and went to sleep happy, for the sacred flame would burn for another year and it was Easter Day.

from *A Window on Greece*

# EASTER MONDAY

## Children's Egg Rolling in the United States

The eggs were originally rolled down the terrace of the Capitol grounds; but later on the White House lawn.

At first the children sit sedately in long rows; each had brought a basket of gay-coloured hard-boiled eggs, and those on the upper terraces send them rolling to the line next below, and those pass on the ribbon-like streams to other hundreds at the foot, who scramble for the hopping eggs and hurry panting to the top to start them rolling down again. And as the sport wanes, those on top who have rolled all the eggs they brought, finally roll themselves, shrieking with laughter. Now comes a swirl of curls, ribbons, and furbelows. Somebody's dainty maid, indifferent to bumps and grass stains. A set of boys, who started in a line of six with joined hands, are trying to come down in somersaults without breaking the chain. On all sides,

68

the older folk stand by to watch the games of this infant carnival.

In 1921, during the administration of President Harding, the gates opened at nine in the morning and remained open till five in the afternoon. Thousands of children rolled 300,000 eggs. The children whose eggs weren't cracked were the winners.

As no adult was allowed in the grounds unless accompanied by a child, some commercially-minded boys escorted adults into the grounds for fifteen cents, and then went outside to find others who wished to see the sport close at hand.

from The American Book of Days

April

# APRIL 1st

## All Fools' Day

The first of April, some do say,
Is set apart for All Fools' Day.
But why the people call it so,
Nor I, nor they themselves, do know.

The keeping of All Fools' Day is very widespread and ancient. In France it is called *Poisson d'Avril* (April Fish); in India it takes place on March 31st, and is called *Huli*. Some say that the custom of making April fools comes from the Roman Festival Cereali, commemorating Ceres. When Ceres's daughter, Proserpine, was in the Elysian meadows with her lap full of daffodils, Pluto, god of the underworld, came and carried her off. Proserpine screamed, Ceres ran to help her. But instead of following her screams, she followed the *echo* of them, the Elysian meadows being among the mountains. So she ran in the wrong direction. And thus was fooled.

Here are some April Fool tricks:

1 Ask a child to go to a dairy and buy some pigeon's milk.
2 Ask a child to go to a bookshop and buy a *Life of Eve's Mother*.
3 *Small boy* (stopping lady in the street): 'Ma'am, I beg your pardon, but you've something on your face.'
   *Lady*: 'What is it, boy?'
   *Small boy*: 'Your nose, ma'am. April fool!'

# The Bright Weather Festival

## *Chiang Yee*

*Ch'ing* means clear and *ming* means bright, and Ch'ing-ming signifies weather suitable for going out into the countryside. Appropriately, the Ching-ming Festival took place at the end of April or the beginning of May. It was the occasion chosen to carry out the annual family pilgrimage to the ancestral tombs.

In my family the age at which one was first allowed to join the pilgrimage was about twelve. This was for the practical reason that the family cemetery lay a long way off in the hills and the journey had to be done on foot, since there was no other means of transport save sedan chairs, which were only hired for grandparents and other elderly members.

Preparations began about ten days beforehand. First one of the elders bought many large sheets of coloured paper, which the ladies made into *Fen-piao*, 'grave banners'. They cut the paper into strips and wound the strips round a stick, changing the colour frequently. At the top they fixed a long pennon of paper which waved in the wind when the stick was set up on the tomb, indicating that descendants of the deceased had visited the spot. Fresh flowers were never placed on tombs, and banners were only placed there once a year.

Like other young people of my family I went on my first pilgrimage at about the age of twelve, and, like them I am sure, my first impressions will always be vivid in my memory. My grandparents being unable to go, my third great-uncle took charge of the party. Not all the elders could leave home, and the aunts could not walk the distance on their small feet. Finally, apart from any number of my generation, just my father and two uncles supported the third great-uncle. We all set out at the same time but presently split up into three groups to visit our respective cemeteries. I followed my father, who was

74

with the third great-uncle. The two uncles led the other groups. Before separating, the third great-uncle arranged for us all to meet at a village half-way between Kiu-kiang and Lu mountain, where there was a good inn.

It was a lovely day, neither hot nor cold. The sun shone brightly, with intermittent drizzling showers. All the hills were green. The fields were planted with *yiu-tsai*, a plant with a group of tiny yellow flowers at the top of each stem; whole stretches of the countryside were carpeted with yellow. In some fields the young sprouts of wheat and rice were showing. The figures of farmers could be seen here and there; some were still sowing, some leading the buffalo out to plough, some singing *shan-ke* (hill songs) with a long-drawn intonation while they worked. This and the songs of birds were the only sounds to be heard. In the quiet we could even hear the tiny hissing of the mild wind in the leaves and grasses. Nearly every hut or cottage we passed had some apricot- or peach-trees in bloom, and by the streams the willows were all fresh in their new green robes. Petals of apricot or peach blossom floated idly on the surface of the water, and the tiny white feathery flowers of the willows hovered in the air. Two famous lines by one of our best-known poets might have been written to describe the scene:

> Touches my clothes as if to make them wet, the apricot rain.
> Blows on my face but not cold, the willow wind.

By closing my eyes I can still recall all the colours I saw, yellow, green, pink and white, and sometimes small red spots here and there where country girls in red frocks or trousers emerged from their cottages or walked along the hedges. Most of the people we passed looked very happy and jolly, talking and laughing all the time. We exchanged greetings with them and sometimes had to enquire the direction from farmers. I was always pleased when we mistook our way, because then

75

we could have a good laugh and turn back. This innocent joy, and the whole happy atmosphere, is very difficult to describe. Occasionally, however, we met some pilgrim who, having suffered a recent loss, looked sad.

I was allowed to sit in the third great-uncle's sedan chair now and then when he wanted to walk for a change. But actually he told us so many stories of the countryside and pointed out so many interesting trees and herbs that I forgot to be tired. . . .

The tombs which our group was going to visit were scattered on two hills. One of the tombs held the ancestor who had first moved our family from northern China to Kiu-kiang. We youngsters busily unpacked the banners and dishes. We set a few banners on this tomb first and laid the dishes before it. Then we burnt incense and each of us in order of age knelt before the tomb. On one side was a stone tablet with the name of the dead and the dates of his birth and death, together with those of his wife; also a very brief account of how he had moved the family. Then we proceeded to the other tombs. My mother's was on the other hill. Father took my brother and sister and me to it while the rest of the group rested in a cottage. On the way I asked why we had not come to Mother's tomb first. Father explained that the older ancestor had to be honoured first. Though Father spoke the words very seriously, I still felt that my mother was my most important ancestor. But the gravity of Father's face prevented me from asking any further questions. When we reached Mother's tomb Father remarked how well the plants round it were growing. Most of the pines and other trees had been planted by Father himself at the time of Mother's burial. Farther down the slope of the hills were masses of wild azaleas, and the contrast of deep red and green made a beautiful picture. Father seemed very pleased with the scenery but he sighed deeply at times. After burning incense and letting off crackers Father bowed to the tomb three times, but we youngsters, the children of the deceased, knelt down

76

and bowed our heads to the ground three times. Father did not speak except to tell us to read the inscription on the tombstone tablet. We were all silent for a while.

Presently we returned to the cottage. It was the duty of the people who occupied it to tend our tombs. My third great-uncle gave them renewed instructions and Father added a special word about Mother's tomb. Before leaving we picked a few branches of pine, peach and willow as well as a few azaleas to indicate that our ancestors would protect us and keep us as fresh and pure as these branches, which were, at the same time, tokens of spring to take back home.

After a couple of hours we reached the inn, where the other two groups had already arrived. The inn was full. Many other people had picked the same kind of branches as ourselves. People talked to each other as if they were old acquaintances. Father ordered the dishes for all of us and we had a good meal. I kept very silent partly because I was rather tired and partly because I liked to watch the jolly red faces around me. My third great-uncle teased me for being tired, but I defended myself by saying that I was quite able to walk home. We got back at dusk.

from *A Chinese Childhood*

# APRIL 23rd

# Saint George's Day

Saint George is the patron saint of England, and in most people's minds is immediately associated with a dragon. This dragon, so legend tells us, lived in a pond outside the town of Silene in Libya; and unless he was given plenty of sheep to eat, he would come out of his pond, prance up to the town walls,

and kill the townsfolk with his poisonous breath. When the people of Silene ran out of sheep, they took to offering their daughters to the dragon. The girls were chosen by lot, and one day the lot fell to the King's daughter. The dragon was just scrambling out of his pond to devour her, when a Christian knight, called George, came riding by. Making the sign of the

cross, he charged the dragon with his lance, and the dragon fell
to the ground. George then told the princess to tie her girdle
round this most discomfited dragon, and lead it to the town,
which she did.

By this miracle the King and all the citizens were converted
to Christianity. But, later, George was tortured and put to

79

death by the heathen emperor, Diocletian. So he became *Saint* George the Martyr, and was idolized in many eastern countries. And when the Crusaders returned from the East, they brought back with them such glowing stories of Saint George's valour and piety, that he was chosen as the patron saint of England; and 'God and Saint George!' became England's battle cry.

In former times Saint George's Day was celebrated in English towns and villages by pageants in which a gallant Saint George, armour-clad and riding a noble charger, and a fearsome dragon with snapping jaws, were the principal performers:

'Who that has seen a Norwich Guild procession, twenty years ago, does not remember *Snap-Snap*? The terror and delight of children, the representation of the Dragon, which used to be borne at the head of the procession, opening wide its jaws to receive contributions. The man who walked under the scaly hide flourished the long forked tail, and pulled the string which moved the dreadful head and jaws,' wrote a contributor to the *Edinburgh Review*.

But that was over a hundred years ago and in these latter days such pageants have more or less died out.

However, there is one celebration that is still kept up on this day, and increases in importance year by year; and that is the festival held at Stratford-on-Avon, Shakespeare's birthplace. On this day pilgrimages are made to the little town from all over the world, and the flags of all nations are unfurled at noon in the principal street. For Shakespeare was born in Stratford-on-Avon in April 1564, and though the day of his birth is not certain, it is believed to be the 23rd. And he died on April 23rd in 1616.

It is pleasant to think that England's saint and England's greatest poet hold their festivals on the same day.

May

# Sister Awake!

## Thomas Bateman

Sister awake! close not your eyes!
The day her light discloses,
And the bright morning doth arise
        Out of her bed of roses.

See the clear sun, the world's bright eye,
In at our window peeping:
Lo, how he blusheth to espy
Us idle wenches sleeping!

Therefore awake! make haste, I say,
And let us, without staying,
All in our gowns of green so gay
Into the Park a-maying!

# May Day

## Flora Thompson

At last came spring and spring brought May Day, the greatest
day in the year from the children's point of view.
    The May garland was all that survived there of the old May

Day festivities. The maypole and the May games and May dances in which whole parishes had joined had long been forgotten. Beyond giving flowers for the garland and pointing out how things should be done the older people took no part in the revels.

The foundation of the garland was a light wooden framework of uprights supporting graduated hoops, forming a bell-shaped structure about four feet high. This frame was covered with flowers, bunched and set closely after the manner of wreath-making.

On the last morning of April the children would come to school with bunches, baskets, arms and pinafores full of flowers – every blossom they could find in the fields and hedges or beg from parents and neighbours . . . Primroses . . . violets from the hedgerows, cowslips from the meadows, and wall-flowers, oxlips, and sprays of pale red flowering currant from the cottage gardens formed the main supply. A sweetbriar hedge in the schoolmistress's garden furnished unlimited greenery.

In time the wooden frame was covered, even if there had to be solid greenery to fill up at the back, out of sight. Then the 'Top-knot', consisting of a bunch of crown imperial, yellow and brown, was added to crown the whole, and the fragrant, bowery structure was sprinkled with water and set aside for the night.

While the garland was being dressed, an older girl, perhaps the May Queen herself, would be busy in a corner making a crown. This always had to be a daisy crown; but, meadow daisies being considered too common . . . garden daisies, white and red, were used, with a background of dark, glossy, evergreen leaves.

The May Queen had been chosen weeks beforehand. She was supposed to be either the prettiest or the most popular girl in the parish; but it was more often a case of self-election by the strongest-willed or of taking turns: 'You choose me this year and I'll choose you next'. However elected, the queens had a strong resemblance to each other, being stout-limbed, rosy-cheeked maidens of ten or eleven, with great manes of dark hair frizzed out to support the crown becomingly.

The final touches were given to the garland when the children assembled at six o'clock on May Day morning. Then a large china doll in a blue frock was brought forth from the depths of the school needlework chest and arranged in a sitting position on a little ledge in the centre front of the garland. This doll was known as 'the lady', and a doll of some kind was considered essential. It was understood that the garland was her garland, carried in her honour. The lady must never be roughly handled. If the garland turned turtle, as it was apt to do later in the day, when the road was rough and the bearers were growing weary, the first question was always 'Is the lady all right?' (Is it possible that the lady was once 'Our Lady', she having in her turn, perhaps, replaced an earlier effigy of some pagan spirit of the newly-decked earth?)

The lady comfortably settled in front of the garland, a large white muslin veil or skirt was draped over the whole to act as a drop-scene and sunshade combined. Then a broomstick was inserted between the hoops for carrying purposes.

All the children in the parish between the ages of seven and eleven were by this time assembled, those girls who possessed them wearing white or light-coloured frocks, and girls and boys alike decked out with bright ribbon knots and bows and sashes, those of the boys worn crosswise over one shoulder. The Queen wore her daisy crown with a white veil thrown over it, and the other girls who could procure them also wore white veils. White gloves were traditional, but could seldom be obtained. . . .

The procession then formed. It was as follows:

Boy with flag                     Girl with money box
             The GARLAND with two bearers
                    King and Queen

84

Two maids of honour
Lord and Lady
Two maids of honour
Footman and footman's lady
Rank and file, walking in twos
Girl known as 'Mother'          Boy called 'Ragman'

The 'Mother' was one of the most dependable of the older girls, who was made responsible for the behaviour of the garlanders. She carried a large, old-fashioned, double-lidded marketing basket over her arm, containing the lunches of the principal actors. The boy called 'Ragman' carried the coats, brought in case of rain, but seldom worn, even during a shower, lest by their poverty and shabbiness they should disgrace the festive attire.

The procession stepped out briskly. Mothers waved and implored their offspring to behave well; some of the little ones left behind lifted up their voices and wept; old people came to cottage gates and said that, though well enough, this year's procession was poor compared to some they had seen. But the garlanders paid no heed, they had their feet on the road at last and vowed they would not turn back now, 'not if it rained cats and dogs'.

The first stop was at the rectory, where the garland was planted before the front door and the shrill little voices struck up, shyly at first, but gathering confidence as they went on:

> A bunch of May I have brought you
> And at your door it stands.
> It is but a sprout, but it's well put about
> By the Lord Almighty's hand.
>
> God bless the master of this house
> God bless the mistress too,
> And all the little children
> That round the table go.

And now I've sung my short little song
I must no longer stay.
God bless you all, both great and small,
And send you a happy May Day.

During the singing of this the rector's face, wearing its mildest expression, and bedaubed with shaving lather, for it was only as yet seven o'clock, would appear at an upper window and nod approval and admiration of the garland. His daughter would be down and at the door, and for her the veil was lifted and the glory of the garland revealed. She would look, touch and smell, then slip a silver coin into the money box, and the procession would move on towards the squire's.

There, the lady of the house would bow haughty approval, and if there were visiting grandchildren the lady would be detached from the garland and held up to their nursery window to be admired. Then the squire himself would appear in the stable doorway with a brace of sniffing, suspicious spaniels at his heels. 'How many are there of you?' he would call. 'Twenty-seven? Well, here's a five-bob bit for you. Don't quarrel over it. Now let's have a song.'

'Not *A Bunch of May*,' the girl called Mother would whisper, impressed by the five-shilling piece; not that old-fashioned thing. Something newer, and something newer, though still not so very new, would be selected. Perhaps it would be:

All hail gentle spring
With thy sunshine and showers,
And welcome the sweet buds
That burst in the bowers:

Again we rejoice as thy light step and free
Brings leaves to the woodland and flowers to the bee,
Bounding, bounding, bounding, bounding,
Joyful and gay,
Light and airy, like a fairy,
Come, come away.

Or it might be:

Come see our new garland so green and so gay;
'Tis the firstfruits of spring and the glory of May.
Here are cowslips and daisies and hyacinths blue,
Here are buttercups bright and anemones too.

During the singing of the latter song, as each flower was mentioned, a specimen would be pointed to in the garland. It was always a point of honour to have at least one of each named in the several verses. . . .

After becoming duty had been paid to the rectory and big house, the farmhouse and cottages were visited; then the little procession set out along narrow, winding country roads, with tall hedges of blackthorn and bursting leaf-buds on either side, to make its seven-mile circuit. In those days there were no motors to dodge and there was very little other traffic; just a farm cart here and there, or the baker's white-tilted van, or a governess car with nurses and children out for their airing. Sometimes the garlanders would forsake the road for stiles and footpaths across buttercup meadows, or go through parks and gardens to call at some big house or secluded farmstead.

In the ordinary course, country children of that day seldom went beyond their own parish bounds, and this long trek opened up new country to most of them. There was a delightful element of exploration about it. New short cuts would be tried, one year through a wood, another past the fishponds, or across such and such a paddock, where there might, or might not, be a bull. On one pond they passed sailed a solitary swan; on the terrace before one mansion peacocks spread their tails in the sun. There were often showers, and to Laura, looking back after fifty years, the whole scene would melt into a blur of wet greenery, with rainbows and cuckoo-calls and, overpowering all other impressions, the wet wallflower and primrose scent of the May garland.

from *Lark Rise to Candleford*

87

# Corinna's Going A-Maying

## *Robert Herrick*

Get up, get up, for shame! The blooming morn
Upon her wings presents the god unshorn.
See how Aurora throws her fair
Fresh-quilted colours through the air:
Get up, sweet slug-a-bed, and see
The dew bespangling herb and tree!
Each flower has wept and bow'd toward the east
Above an hour since, yet you are not drest;
Nay! not so much as out of bed?
When all the birds have matins said
And sung their thankful hymns, 'tis sin,
Nay profanation to keep in,
Whereas a thousand virgins on this day
Spring sooner than the lark, to fetch in May.

Come, my Corinna, come; and coming, mark
How each field turns a street, each street a park,
Made green and trimm'd with trees! see how
Devotion gives each house a bough
Or branch! each porch, each door, ere this,
An ark, a tabernacle is,
Made up of whitethorn neatly interwove,
As if here were those cooler shades of love.
Can such delights be in the street
And open fields, and we not see't?
Come, we'll abroad! and let's obey
The proclamation made for May,
And sin no more, as we have done, by staying;
But, my Corinna, come, let's go a-Maying.

# The Padstow Hobby Horse

## *Ruth Manning-Sanders*

On the first day of May the inhabitants of the little fishing
town of Padstow in Cornwall are early astir. For on this day
the Hobby Horse comes rollicking out of the Red Lion Inn
to bring the summer and the May into every house and
cottage. The man who represents this horse wears a huge hoop-
shaped frame covered with black tarpaulin, and a fierce mask
with red eyes.

*Hipperty-skip!* Off through the streets of the town he prances,
accompanied by his Teaser, dressed in motley and carrying a
cardboard club, and also by a man dressed as a woman, called
All Sorts, and two musicians. The crowds are thick in the
narrow streets – and how they sing! The whole town resounds
with the lovely tune of the Night Song:

> Unite and unite, and let us all unite,
> (For Summer is a-come unto day,)
> And whither we are going we all will unite,
> In the merry morning of May.
>
> The young men of Padstow they might if they would,
> (For Summer is a-come unto day,)
> They might have built a ship and gilt her all with gold
> In the merry morning of May.
>
> The maidens of Padstow they might if they would.
> (For Summer is a-come unto day,)
> They might have made a garland with the white rose and
>      the red,
> In the merry morning of May.

Where are the maidens that here now should sing?
(For Summer is a-come unto day,)
They are in the meadows the flowers a-gathering,
In the merry morning of May.

Young women carrying flowers and branches now join the little procession:

'Oss, Oss, we Oss!' cry the crowd. And thus encouraged the Hobby picks out a pretty girl, and whilst she shrieks and struggles, gets her against a wall and 'capes' her. That is, he turns his back, lifts his hood and brings it down over her head. And if the inside of the hood is smeared with blacklead and leaves its mark on the girl's face, that is all the better, for it brings good luck to her throughout the year.

Later on the crowd changes its singing into the Day Song, with its mysterious words, and slower, but no less beautiful tune:

Where is Saint George? Oh where is *he*, O?
He is out in his long-boat, all on the salt *sea*, O.
Up flies the kite, and down falls the lark, O.
Aunt Ursula Birdwood she had an old ewe,
And she died in her own Old Park, O!

Whilst this is being sung the Hobby Horse collapses: he falls flat on the ground. But the Teaser strokes Hobby's head with his cardboard club. Hobby springs into life again, leaps up and capers wildly. Yes, he has died and been revived, and the crowd encourages him with yet another song:

Up Merry Spring, and up the merry ring,
(For Summer is a-come unto day,)
How happy are those little birds that merrily do sing
On the merry morning of May.

So it goes on all through the merry day, until twilight falls, and through the darkling streets the last song echoes:

Now fare you well and we bid you all good cheer,
(For Summer is a-come unto day,)
We'll call no more unto your house before another year,
In the merry morning of May.

And after that comes night and silence.

June

# A Village Peace Festival

## *Laurie Lee*

The first big festival that I can remember was Peace Day in 1919. It was a day of magical transformations, of tears and dusty sunlight, of bands, processions, and buns by the cartload; and I was so young I thought it normal. . . .

We had all been provided with fancy dress, and that seemed normal too. . . .

On the morning of the feast Poppy Green came to the house to try on her angel's dress. She was five years old and about my size. She had russet curls like apple peelings, a polished pumpkin face, a fruity air of exploding puddings, and a perpetual cheeky squint. I loved her, she was like a portable sweetshop. This morning I watched my sisters dress her. She was supposed to represent a spirit. They'd made her a short frilly frock, a tinfoil helmet, cardboard wings, and a wand with a star. When they'd clothed her they stood her up on the mantelpiece and had a good look at her. Then went off awhile on some other business and left us alone together.

'Fly!' I commanded. 'You got wings, ain't you?'
Poppy squirmed and wiggled her shoulders.

I grew impatient and pushed her off the mantelpiece, and she fell with a howl into the fireplace. Looking down at her, smudged with coal and tears, her wand and wings all crumpled, I felt nothing but rage and astonishment. She should have been fluttering round the room.

94

They sponged her and soothed her, and Poppy trotted home, her bent wand clutched in her hand. Then shapes and phantoms began to run through the village, and we started to get ready ourselves. Marge appeared as Queen Elizabeth, with Phyllis her lady-in-waiting. Marjorie, who was sixteen and at her most beautiful, wore a gown of ermine, a brocaded bodice, and a black cap studded with pearls. She filled the kitchen with such a glow of grace that we just stood and gaped at her. It was the first time I had seen Queen Elizabeth, but this was no sharp-faced Tudor. Tender and proud in her majestic robes, she was the Queen of Heaven, risen from the dust, unrecognizable as Marge till she spoke, and her eyes shone down on us from her veils of ermine like emeralds laid in snow. Phyllis, in finery of her own, skipped like a magpie around her, wearing a long chequered dress of black and white velvet, and a hat full of feathers and moths.

The rest of us, whom Marjorie had dressed, were the result of homespun inspirations. Dorothy as 'Night', was perhaps the most arresting; and apparition of unearthly beauty, a flash of darkness, a strip of nocturnal sky, mysteriously cloaked in veils of black netting entangled with silver paper. A crescent moon lay across her breast, a comet across her brow, and her long dark curls fell in coils of midnight and were sprinkled with tinsel dust. I smelt frost when I saw her and heard a crackling of stars; familiar Dorothy had grown far and disturbing.

Brother Jack had refused to be dressed up at all, unless in some aspect of recognized valour. So they hung him in green, gave him a bow and arrow, and he called himself Robin Hood. Little Tony was dressed as a market-girl, curly-headed and pretty as love, bare-armed and bonneted, carrying a basket of flowers, but so proud that we forgave him his frock.

As for me, a squat neck and solid carriage made the part I should play inevitable. I was John Bull – whoever he was – but I quickly surmised his importance. I remember the girls stuffing me into my clothes with many odd squeals and giggles.

95

Gravely I offered an arm or leg, but remained dignified and aloof . . . I wore a top hat and choker, a Union Jack waistcoat, a frock-coat, and pillowcase breeches. But I'd been finished off hurriedly with gaiters of cardboard fastened loosely together with pins – a slovenly makeshift which offended my taste, and which I was never able to forgive.

This Peace Day I remember as a blur of colour, leading from fury to triumph. There was a procession with a band. I walked alone solemnly. Fantastic disguises surrounded me; every single person seemed covered with beards, false noses, boot-black and wigs. We had not marched far when my boots fell off, followed by my cardboard gaiters. As I stopped to find them, the procession swept over me. I sat down by the roadside and howled. I howled because I could hear the band disappear-ing, because I was John Bull and it should not have happened. I was picked up by a carriage, restored to the procession, then placed on a trolley and pulled. Cross-legged on the trolley, bare-footed and gaiterless, I rode like a prince through the village.

Dusty, sweating from its long route-march, the procession snaked round the houses. The old and infirm stood and cheered from the gutters; I nodded back from my trolley. At last we entered the cool beech wood through which the squire's drive twisted. The brass band's thunder bounced back from the boughs. Owls hooted and flapped away.

We came out of the wood into the Big House gardens, and the sun returned in strength. Doves and pigeons flew out of the cedars. The swans took off from the lake. On the steps of the Manor stood the wet-eyed squire, already in tears at the sight of us. His mother, in a speech from a basket-chair, mentioned the glory of God, the Empire, us; and said we wasn't to touch the flowers.

With that the procession dispersed, I was tipped off the trolley, and I wandered away through the grounds. Flags and roses moved against the sky, bright figures among the bushes.

Japanese girls and soot-faced savages grew strangely from banks of lilac. I saw Charlie Chaplin, Peter the Pieman, a collection of upright tigers, a wounded soldier about my own age, and a bride on the arm of a monkey.

Later I was given a prize by the squire, and was photographed in a group by a rockery. I still have that picture, all sepia shadows, a leaf ripped from that summer day. Surrounded by girls in butter muslin, by Druids and eastern kings, I am a figure rooted in unshakable confidence, oval, substantial and proud. About two feet high and two feet broad, my breeches like slack balloons, I stand top-hatted, with a tilted face as severe as on a Roman coin. Others I recognize are gathered round me, all marked by that day's white dust. Tony has lost his basket of flowers, Jack his bow and arrows. Poppy Green has had her wings torn off and is grasping a broken lily. She stands beside me, squinting fiercely, ruffled a bit by the heat, and the silver letters across her helmet – which I couldn't read then – say PEACE.

from *Cider with Rosie*

# JUNE 23rd AND 24th

# Midsummer Eve and Day

Midsummer Eve is a time of magic. Then the fairies are abroad, and the witches also. The witches go flying on their broomsticks, or riding on black cats through the air, to gather on the high hills, there to meet the Devil and swear their allegiance to him. On these high hills they light their fire, and dance round it, keeping their backs to the fire, and their faces turned towards night. Meanwhile there is a wild hunt going on in the sky above them, where spectral hunters career on spectral steeds, surrounded by spectral dogs.

This is the night, too, to gather fernseed, which, when put in the shoe, has the power of making its lucky owner invisible, and of guiding him to hidden treasure. But you must not touch the seed with your hand nor let it fall to the ground; you must catch it as it falls in a white handkerchief, and from the handkerchief shake it into your shoe. However, very few among mortals are the owners of this much coveted fernseed; the witches do all in their power to prevent anyone catching it. No, they don't approve of mortals possessing magic power.

There is another magical plant, the springwort, that grows in Germany in the Hartz mountains, and only blooms underneath a fern, between 11 and 12 at night on Midsummer Eve. When the bell tolls twelve, it vanishes. The flower is yellow and shines like a lamp, and it goes hopping about and is never still for a moment. It is afraid of men, and if it sees a man it runs away. But if a man can pounce, catch it, and put it in his right-hand pocket, he can never more be wounded by knife or bullet. Also it has the power to unlock all doors, and is therefore a treasure-trove for thieves.

Fires were, and still are in some places, lit on the tops of hills on Midsummer Eve. In Cornwall, especially, a chain of fires blazes out from hill to hill across the whole county. When the blaze dies down, girls and youths take hands and jump over the embers to bring them good luck; and formerly cattle were driven across the embers to cure them of any sickness, and to keep them in health till Midsummer comes round again.

By Midsummer Eve the days have begun to shorten and the nights to lengthen, and perhaps these fires, which are certainly a legacy from pagan times, are to hearten us against a feeling of dismay at the lessening of Earth's light, and a human defiance of the power of darkness.

# Midsummer in Bullerby

## *Astrid Lindgren*

And now I want to tell you what we did on Midsummer Eve, the 23rd of June. In the South Farm meadow we had a Midsummer pole (we always have one in Sweden.) Everybody in the whole village helped to make it.

First we rode way out into the forest in our wagon to pick the leaves that we were going to use. Father drove, and even Kerstin (the baby) was allowed to come along. She was so happy that she laughed and laughed. Olaf gave her a little branch to hold in her hand, and she sat and waved it back and forth. And Olaf sang this old song for her:

> 'Kerstin had a little gold coach
> In which she was going to ride;
> A little gold whip she held in the air
> And smiled on the world with pride . . .'

All the rest of us sang too. Agda had come along to help us pick leaves and she sang:

> 'Now it is summer;
> Now there is sunshine,
> Now there are flowers and leaves . . .'

When we came home from the forest, Agda, Britta, Anna and I picked a big bunch of lilacs from the bushes behind our woodshed. Then we took them over to the South Farm meadow, where Oscar and Kalle had already cut the pole. We tied the leaves all round the pole and hung two big wreaths of lilacs from the crossbar at the top. Then we raised the pole and danced round it.

Uncle Eric, Anna's father, plays the accordion well, and he played a lot of gay tunes for us all to dance to – all except

100

*On these high hills they light their fire,*
*and dance round it*

Grandpa and Kerstin. Grandpa sat in a chair and Kerstin sat in his lap at first. But she couldn't stop pulling his beard, so her daddy put her up on his shoulders. In that way, Kerstin could dance with us too.

Poor Grandpa couldn't dance, but I don't think he was sorry. He just said, 'My, oh my, it seems longer ago than yesterday that I danced round a Midsummer pole!'

Then we all sat down in the grass and drank coffee that Mother and Aunt Gretta and Aunt Lisa had made. We had buns and cake too. Grandpa drank three cups of coffee, because that's something he really likes.

'Coffee is something I have to have,' he says.

I don't like it at all, but when you drink it while sitting in the grass at Midsummer, it tastes better than usual.

We played 'The last pair out' and a lot of other games. It's such fun when the mothers and fathers play with us. It would probably not be so much fun if we had to play with them every day, but when it's Midsummer, I think they should be allowed to play too.

Svipp ran round and barked while we played. I think he thought it was fun too.

We were allowed to stay up just as long as we wanted to that evening. Agda said if you climbed over nine fences before you went to bed, and if you picked nine kinds of flowers and put them under your pillow, you'd dream at night about the one you would marry.

Britta and Anna and I thought it would be lots of fun to climb over nine fences, although we already know who we are going to marry. I'm going to marry Olaf and Britta and Anna are going to marry Lars and Pip.

'Are you going to climb over nine fences?' Lars said to Britta. 'Well, go ahead, by all means. But please dream about someone else and not me. Not that I'm superstitious, but it *might* help.'

'Yes, let's hope you don't dream about us,' Pip said.

'Yes, let's *certainly* hope so,' Olaf said.

The boys are stupid and don't want to marry us.

Agda said that you had to be very quiet while you climbed over the fences. You couldn't laugh or talk at all the whole time.

'If you can't talk the whole time, Lisa,' Lars said, 'then you might just as well go to bed.'

'Why?' I said.

'Because you can't climb nine fences in two minutes, and you've never been quiet longer than that in your life – except the time you had mumps, of course.'

We didn't pay any attention to the boys, but just started climbing. We began with the fence round South Farm meadow and came into the birch woods behind it.

It's strange in the woods when it's dark. Well, it wasn't perfectly dark, just rather twilightish and still. It was very quiet, because the birds had stopped chirping, and it smelled so good because of all the trees and flowers. We each picked a flower when we had climbed over the first fence.

There is one thing that I don't understand, and that's why you always get the giggles when you know that you're not supposed to laugh. As soon as we had climbed over the first fence, we started.

The boys came climbing after us just to tease us and make us laugh.

'Don't step in the mud puddle,' Pip said to Anna.

'There's no puddle –' Anna said. But then she remembered that she wasn't supposed to talk. Then Britta and Anna and I giggled and the boys laughed out loud.

'You can't giggle like that,' Lars said. 'Remember that you're not supposed to laugh.'

Then we giggled still more. And the boys ran round us and pulled our hair and pinched our arms to make us laugh. We couldn't say anything because we weren't supposed to talk.

'Ubbelibubblelimuck,' Lars said.

103

It wasn't a bit funny, really, but Britta and Anna and I couldn't keep from laughing. I stuffed my handkerchief into my mouth, but that didn't help; my laughter came chirping out all the same. But when we had climbed over the ninth fence, and picked our ninth flower, we stopped laughing and were just mad at the boys for spoiling everything for us.

But even though I was angry with the boys I put the flowers under my pillow. I had a buttercup and a bluebell and a daisy and an almond flower and a rockrose and a violet and two other flowers that I don't know the names of. I didn't dream of anything at all that night, and I'm certain that it was because those silly boys had made us laugh.

But I'm going to marry Olaf anyway, so there!

from *Cherry Time at Bullerby*

July

# JULY 4th

# Independence Day

## *Laura Ingalls Wilder*

Almanzo was eating breakfast before he remembered that this was the Fourth of July.

It was like Sunday morning. After breakfast he scrubbed his face with soft soap till it shone, and he parted his wet hair and combed it sleekly down. He put on his sheep's-grey trousers and his shirt of French calico, and his vest and his short round coat . . .

He put on his round straw hat, which Mother had made of braided oat-straws, and he was all dressed up for Independence Day. He felt very fine.

Father's shining horses were hitched to the shining red-wheeled buggy, and they all drove away in the cool sunshine. All the country had a holiday air. Nobody was working in the fields, and along the road the people in their Sunday clothes were driving to town.

(In the town) all the stores were closed, but ladies and gentlemen were walking up and down and talking. Ruffled little girls carried parasols, and all the boys were dressed up, like Almanzo. Flags were everywhere, and in the Square the band was playing 'Yankee Doodle'. The fifes tooted and the flutes shrilled and the drums came in with rub-a dub-dub.

Yankee Doodle went to town
Riding on a pony,
He stuck a feather in his hat,
And called it macaroni.

Even the grown-ups had to keep time to it. And there, in the corner of the Square, were the two brass cannons!

The Square was not really square. The railroad made it three-cornered. But everybody called it the Square, anyway. It was fenced, and grass grew there. Benches stood in rows on the grass, and the people were filing between the benches and sitting down as they did in church. . . .

The band stopped playing and the minister prayed. Then the band tuned up again and everybody rose. Men and boys took off their hats. The band played and everybody sang:

'Oh say, can you see by the dawn's early light,
What so proudly we hailed at the twilight's last gleaming,
Whose broad stripes and bright stars through the perilous
    night,
O'er the ramparts we watched were so gallantly
    streaming?'

From the top of the flagpole, up against the blue sky, the Stars and Stripes were fluttering. Everybody looked at the American flag, and Almanzo sang with all his might.

Then everybody sat down, and a congressman stood up on the platform. Slowly and solemnly he read the Declaration of Independence:

'When in the course of human events it became necessary for one people . . . to assume among the powers of the earth the separate and equal station . . . We hold these truths to be self-evident, that all men are created equal . . .'

Almanzo felt solemn and very proud.
. . . All the flags were fluttering, and everybody was happy,

because they were all free and independent, and this was Independence Day. And it was time to eat dinner.

[Almanzo and his family have a picnic lunch on the grass in the churchyard. Then they go back to the Square to watch the firing of the two cannons.]

. . . The band came marching down the street, and they all ran along beside it. The flag was gloriously waving in front, then came the buglers blowing, and the fifers tootling and the drummer rattling the drumstick on the drum. Up the street and down the street went the band, with all the boys following it, and then it stopped in the Square by the brass cannons.

The cannons sat on their haunches, pointing their long barrels upward. The band kept on playing. Two men kept shouting, 'Stand back! Stand back!' and other men were pouring black powder into the cannons' muzzles and pushing it down with wads of cloth on long rods. . . .

Then all the boys ran to pull grass and weeds along the railroad track. They carried them by armfuls to the cannons, and the men crowded the weeds into the cannons' muzzles and drove them down with the long rods.

A bonfire was burning by the railroad track, and long iron rods were heating in it . . . Two men took the long iron rods from the fire. Everybody was still, watching. Standing as far from the cannons as they could, the two men stretched out the rods and touched their red-hot tips to the touchholes. A little flame like a candle flame flickered up from the powder. The little flames stood there burning; nobody breathed. Then – BOOM!

The cannons leaped backward, the air was full of flying grass and weeds. Almanzo ran with all the other boys to feel the warm muzzles of the cannons. Everybody was exclaiming about what a loud noise they had made.

'That's the noise that made the Redcoats run!' Mr Paddock said to Father.

'Maybe,' Father said, tugging his beard. 'But it was the

muskets that won the Revolution. And don't forget it was axes and ploughs that made this country.'

'That's so, come to think of it,' Mr Paddock said.

Independence Day was over. The cannons had been fired, and there was nothing more to do but to hitch up the horses and drive home to do the chores.

That night when they were going to the house with the milk, Almanzo asked Father:

'Father, how was it axes and ploughs made this country. Didn't we fight England for it?'

'We fought for Independence, son,' Father said. 'But all the land our forefathers had was a little strip of country here between the mountains and the ocean. All the way west was Indian country, and Spanish and French and English country. It was farmers that took all that country and made it America.'

'How?' Almanzo asked.

'Well, son, the Spaniards were soldiers, and high-and-mighty gentlemen that only wanted gold. And the French were fur-traders, wanting to make quick money. And England was busy fighting wars. But we were farmers, son; we wanted the land. It was farmers that went over the mountains, and cleared the land, and settled it, and farmed it, and hung on to their farms.

'This country goes three thousand miles west now. It goes way out beyond Kansas, and beyond the Great American Desert, over mountains bigger than these mountains, and down to the Pacific Ocean. It's the biggest country in the world, and it was farmers took all that land and made it America, son. Don't you ever forget that.'

from *Farmer Boy*

August

# Holiday Memory

## *Dylan Thomas*

August Bank Holiday . . . in those always radiant, rainless, lazily rowdy and sky-blue summers departed, I remember August Monday from the rising of the sun over the stained and royal town to the husky hushing of the roundabout music and the dowsing of the naphtha jets in the seaside fair; from the bubble-and-squeak to the last of the sandy sandwiches.

There was no need, that holiday morning, for the sluggardly boys to be shouted down to breakfast; out of their jumbled beds they tumbled, scrambled into their rumpled clothes; quickly at the bathroom basin they catlicked their hands and faces, but never forgot to run the water loud and long as though they washed like colliers; in front of the cracked looking-glass bordered with cigarette-cards in their treasure-trove bedrooms, they whisked a gap-tooth comb through their surly hair; and with shining cheeks and noses and tide-marked necks, they took the stairs three at a time.

But for all their scramble and scamper, clamour on the landing, catlick and toothbrush flick, hair-whisk and stair-jump, their sisters were always there before them. Up with the lady lark, they had prinked and frizzed and hot ironed; and smug in their blossoming dresses . . . they were calm; they were virtuous; they had washed their necks; they did not romp or fidget; and only the smallest sister put out her tongue at the noisy boys. . . .

This was the morning when Father, mending one hole in the

thermos flask, made three; when the sun declared war on the butter, and the butter ran; when the dogs, with all the sweet-binned backyards to sniff and bicker in, chased their tails in the jostling kitchen, worried sandshoes, snapped at flies, writhed between legs, scratched among towels, sat smiling on hampers.

And if you could have listened at some of the open doors of some of the houses in the street you might have heard:

'Uncle Owen says he can't find the bottle-opener . . .'

'Has he looked under the hallstand? . . .'

'Willy's cut his finger . . .'

'Got your spade?'

'If somebody doesn't kill that dog . . .'

'Uncle Owen says why should the bottle-opener be under the hallstand?'

'Never again, never again . . .'

'I know I put the pepper somewhere . . .'

'Willy's bleeding . . .'

'Oh come *on*, come on . . .'

'Let's have a look at the bootlace in your bucket . . .'

'If I lay my hands on that dog . . .'

'Uncle Owen's found the bottle-opener . . .'

'Willy's bleeding over the cheese . . .'

And the trams that hissed like ganders took us all to the beautiful beach.

There was cricket on the sand, and sand in the sponge cake, sandflies in the watercress, and foolish, mulish, religious donkeys on the unwilling trot. Girls undressed in slipping tents of propriety; under invisible umbrellas, stout ladies dressed for the male and immoral sea. Little naked navvies dug canals; children with spades and no ambition built fleeting castles; wispy young men, outside the bathing huts, whistled at substantial young women and dogs who desired thrown stones more than the bones of elephants. Recalcitrant uncles huddled over luke ale in the tiger-striped marquees. Mothers in black, like wobbling mountains, gasped under the discarded dresses of daughters who shrilly braved the goblin waves. And fathers, in the once-a-year sun, took fifty winks. Oh, think of all the fifty winks along the paper-bagged sand.

Liquorice Allsorts, and Welsh Hearts, were melting, and the sticks of rock, that we all sucked, were like barbers' poles made of rhubarb.

In the distance, surrounded by disappointed theoreticians and an ironmonger with a drum, a cross man on an orange-box shouted that holidays were wrong.

And the waves rolled on, with rubber ducks and clerks upon them. I remember the patient, laborious, and enamouring hobby, or profession, of burying relatives in the sand.

I remember the princely pastime of pouring sand, from cupped hands or buckets, down collars and tops of dresses; the shriek, the shake, the slap.

I remember the smell of sea and seaweed, wet flesh, wet hair, wet bathing-dresses, the warm smell as of a rabbity field after rain, the smell of pop and splashed sunshades and toffee, the stable-and-straw smell of hot, tossed, tumbled, dug, and trodden sand . . . the smell of vinegar on shelled cockles, winkle smell, shrimp smell, the dripping-oily backstreet winter-smell of chips in newspapers, the smell of ships from the sun-dazed docks round the corner of the sandhills, the smell of the known and paddled-in sea moving, full of the drowned and herrings, out and away and beyond and farther still towards the antipodes that hung their koala-bears and Maoris, kangaroos and boomerangs, upside down over the backs of stars.

And the noise of pummelling Punch, and Judy falling, and a clock tolling or telling no time in the tenantless town; now and again a bell from a lost tower or a train on the lines behind us clearing its throat, and always the hopeless, ravenous swearing and pleading of the gulls, donkey-bray and hawker-cry, harmonicas and toy trumpets, shouting and laughing and singing, hooting of tugs and tramps, the clip of the chair-attendant's puncher, the motor-boat coughing in the bay, and the same hymn and washing of the sea that was heard in the Bible.

'If it could only just, if it could only just?' your lips said again and again, as you scooped in the hob-hot sand . . . 'If it could only just be like this for ever and ever amen.' August Monday all over the earth, from Mumbles where the aunties grew like ladies on a seaside tree to the brown, bear-hugging Henty-land and the turtled Ballantyne Islands. . . .

'Are there donkeys on desert islands?'

'Only sort-of donkeys.'

'What d'you mean, sort-of donkeys?'

'Native donkeys. They hunt things on them!'

'Sort-of walruses and seals and things?'

'Donkeys can't swim.'

'These donkeys can. They swim like whales, they swim like anything, they swim like—'

'Liar.'

'Liar yourself.'

And two small boys fought fiercely and silently in the sand, rolling together in a ball of legs and bottoms.

Then they went and saw the pierrots, or bought vanilla ices.

Lolling or larrikin that unsoiled boiling beauty of a common day, great gods with their braces over their vests, sang, spat pips, puffed smoke at wasps, gulped and ogled, forgot the rent, embraced, posed for the dicky-bird, were coarse, had rainbow-coloured armpits, winked, belched, blamed the radishes, looked at Ilfracombe, played hymns on paper-and-comb, peeled bananas, scratched, found seaweed in their panamas, blew up paper bags and banged them, wished for nothing.

But over all the beautiful beach I remember most the children playing, boys and girls tumbling, moving jewels, who might never be happy again. And 'happy as a sandboy' is true as the heat of the sun.

from *Quite Early One Morning*

115

September

# Harvest Thanksgiving

September is the month in which we hold Thanksgiving services. There is no special date for these services; but there comes a Sunday in the month when the harvest has been gathered in, and the churches and chapels are decorated with fruit and flowers.

# Harvest Home

## Flora Thompson

Harvest time was a natural holiday. 'A hemmed hardworked 'un,' the men would have said: but they all enjoyed the stir and excitement of getting in the crops and their own importance as skilled and trusted workers, with extra beer at the farmer's expense and extra harvest money to follow. . . .

Very early one morning, the men would come out of their houses, pulling on coats and lighting pipes as they hurried and calling to each other with skyward glances, 'Think weather's a-gooin' to hold?' For three weeks or more during harvest the hamlet was astir before dawn and the homely odours of bacon frying, wood fires and tobacco smoke overpowered the pure, damp, earthy scent of the fields. . . .

In the fields where the harvest had begun all was bustle and activity. At that time the mechanical reaper with long, red, revolving arms like windmill sails had already appeared in the locality; but it was looked upon by the men as an auxiliary, a farmers' toy; the scythe still did most of the work, and they did not dream it would ever be superseded. So while the red sails revolved in one field and the youth on the driver's seat of the machine called cheerily to his horses and women followed behind to bind the corn into sheaves, in the next field a band of men would be whetting their scythes and mowing by hand as their fathers had done before them.

With no idea that they were at the end of a long tradition, they still kept up the old country custom of choosing as their leader the tallest and most highly skilled man amongst them, who was then called 'King of the Mowers'. For several harvests in the 'eighties they were led by a man known as Boamer. He had served in the army and was still a fine, well-set-up young fellow with flashing white teeth and a skin darkened by fiercer than English suns.

With a wreath of poppies and green bindweed trails around his wide, rush-plaited hat, he led the band down the swaths as they mowed and decided when and for how long they should halt for a 'breather' and what drinks should be had from the yellow stone jar they kept under the hedge in a shady corner of the field. They did not rest often or long; for every morning they set themselves to accomplish an amount of work in the day that they knew would tax all their powers till long after sunset. 'Set yourself more than you can do and you'll do it' was one of their maxims, and some of their feats in the harvest field astonished themselves as well as the onlooker.

Old Monday, the bailiff, went riding from field to field on his long-tailed grey pony. Not at that season to criticize, but rather to encourage, and to carry strung to his saddle the hooped and handled miniature barrel of beer provided by the farmer.

One of the smaller fields was always reserved for any of the women who cared to go reaping. Formerly all the able-bodied

women not otherwise occupied had gone as a matter of course; but, by the 'eighties, there were only three or four, beside the regular field women, who could handle a sickle. Often the Irish harvesters had to be called in to finish the field.

Patrick, Dominick, James (never called Jim), Big Mike and Little Mike, and Mr O'Hara seemed to the children as much a part of the harvest scene as the corn itself. They came over from Ireland every year to help with the harvest and slept in the farmer's barn, doing their own cooking and washing at a little fire in the open. They were a wild-looking lot, dressed in odd clothes and speaking a brogue so thick that the natives could only catch a word here and there. When not at work, they went about in a band, talking loudly and usually all together, with the purchases they had made at the inn bundled in blue-and-white check handkerchiefs which they carried over their shoulders at the end of a stick. 'Here comes they jabberin' old Irish,' the country people would say, and some of the women pretended to be afraid of them. They could not have been serious, for the Irishmen showed no disposition to harm anyone. All they desired was to earn as much money as possible to send home to their wives, to have enough left to get drunk on a Saturday night, and to be in time for Mass on a Sunday morning. All these aims were fulfilled; for, as the other men confessed, they were 'gluttons for work' and more work meant more money at that season; there was an excellent inn handy, and a Catholic church within three miles.

After the mowing and reaping and binding came the carrying, the busiest time of all. Every man and boy put his best foot forward then, for when the corn was cut and dried it was imperative to get it stacked and thatched before the weather broke. All day and far into the twilight the yellow-and-blue painted farm wagons passed and repassed along the roads between the fields and the stack-yard. Big cart-horses returning with an empty wagon were made to gallop like two-year-olds. Straws hung on the roadside hedges and many a gate-post was

121

*And then suddenly, in a glimmering mist, the*
*whole company sweeps by you and is gone*

knocked down through hasty driving. In the fields the men pitchforked the sheaves to the one who was building the load on the wagon, and the air resounded with 'Hold tights' and 'Wert ups' and 'Who-o-oas'. The hold tight! was no empty cry; sometimes, in the past, the man on top of the load had not held tight or not tight enough. There were tales of fathers and grandfathers whose necks and backs had been broken by a fall from a load, and of other fatal accidents afield, bad cuts from scythes, pitchforks passing through feet, to be followed by lockjaw, and of sunstroke; but, happily, nothing of this kind happened on that particular farm in the 'eighties.

At last, in the cool dusk of evening, the last load was brought in, with a nest of merry boys' faces among the sheaves on the top, and the men walking alongside with pitchforks on shoulders. As they passed along the roads they shouted:

> 'Harvest home! Harvest home!
> Merry, merry, merry harvest home!'

and women came to their cottage gates and waved, and the few passers-by looked up and smiled their congratulations. The joy and pleasure of the labourers in their task well done was pathetic, considering their very small share in the gain. But it was genuine enough; for they still loved the soil and rejoiced in their own work and skill in bringing forth the fruits of the soil, and harvest home put the crown on their year's work.

As they approached the farmhouse their song changed to:

> 'Harvest home! Harvest home!
> Merry, merry, merry harvest home!
> Our bottles are empty, our barrels won't run,
> And we think it's a very dry harvest home.'

and the farmer came out, followed by his daughters and maids with jugs and bottles and mugs, and drinks were handed round amidst general congratulations. Then the farmer invited the men to his harvest home dinner, to be held in a few days' time, and the adult workers dispersed to add up their harvest money and to rest their weary bones. The boys and youths, who could never have too much of a good thing, spent the rest of the evening circling the hamlet and shouting 'Merry, merry, merry harvest home!' until the stars came out and at last silence fell upon the fat rickyard and the stripped fields.

from *Lark Rise to Candleford*

## A Harvest Supper in the 18th Century

### *Richard Cobbold*

Smoking puddings, plain and plum; piles of hot potatoes, cabbages, turnips, carrots and every species of vegetable which the farmer's lands could produce – beef, roast and boiled, mutton, veal and pork, everything good and substantial: a rich custard, apple pies, to which the children did ample justice, for all were seated round this well-furnished table in the old kitchen.

The lord of the feast, or head man in the harvest field, took his seat at the head of the table, whilst the master of the house, and his wife, his sister, and even his daughter, were the servants of the feast. . . .

After the feast, and a flowing jug or two of brown ale had been emptied, the wives and children were invited into the best parlour for tea and cakes, whilst the merry reapers were left · to themselves to enjoy in their own way the stronger harvest ale, which was just broached by the hand of the master.

Then what drinking of toasts to their sweethearts, what singing of songs by this man and that man, the whole company joining to roar out the chorus.

123

Now Will prided himself upon his vocal powers, and was a bold, forward fellow. 'I'll sing you a new song,' says he, 'you can all join in the chorus. I'll sing you *Hallo Largesse*.'
Accordingly he lifted up his voice:

'Now the ripened corn
In sheaves is borne,
And the loaded wain,
Brings home the grain,
The merry, merry reapers sing a bind,
And jocund shouts the happy harvest hind,

Chorus   *Hallo Large! Hallo Large! Hallo Largesse!*

Now the harvest's o'er,
And the grain we store,
And the stacks we pull,
And the barn is full,
The merry, merry reapers sing again,
And jocund shouts the happy harvest swain,

*Hallo Large! Hallo Large! Hallo Largesse!*

Now the feast we share –
'Tis our master's fare,
May he long, long live,
Such a treat to give,
And merry, merry reapers sing with joy,
And jocund shouts the happy harvest boy,

*Hallo Large! Hallo Large! Hallo Largesse!*

Now we join in song,
With our voices strong,
And our hearts are high
With our good supply,
We merry, merry reapers joyful come
To shout and sing our happy Harvest-Home,

*Hallo Large! Hallo Large! Hallo Largesse!*'

[*Largesse*. At harvest, when the men are reaping, should their master have any friends visiting his fields, the head man among the labourers usually asks a *largesse*, which is generally a shilling. At evening, when the work of the day is over, all the men collect in a circle and *Hallo*, that is cry, *Largesse*. Three times they say in a low tone 'Hallo Large!' and all, hand in hand, bow their heads almost to the ground; then they lift their heads, and with one burst of all their voices, cry out *Gesse!*]

from Margaret Catchpole

# SEPTEMBER 29th

## Michaelmas Day

The day of Saint Michael and All Angels has been throughout Christian times a great church festival. Saint Michael is familiar to us as the archangel leader of the heavenly host during that mighty battle which ended with Satan and his rebellious angels being cast down into Hell.

Saint Michael figures in a great many of the 'old masters' paintings. He is winged and haloed, and always in armour, sword in hand: that mighty sword that in Heaven's battle 'smote, and felled squadrons at once'. And there is one dramatic fifteenth-century picture in a Berlin gallery, in which he also holds a pair of scales. He is weighing souls. Under one scale lies a huge devil, in the other scale stands a very small naked soul. The devil has weighted *his* scale with a millstone and other heavy objects, and he clutches the scale in his clawed hands trying to drag it down. But – up flies the devil's scale, down sinks the other. The tiny naked Christian soul triumphantly outweighs the devil and all his works.

October

# A Harvest Festival Procession in Southern India

## Marie Thoger

There was great activity in the stables where the maharajah's elephants were kept. The great white male elephant was being washed and adorned for the festival. On his massive legs huge fantastic flowers were painted in yellow and green, and his toe nails were carefully gilded. The triangular ornament studded with precious stones was polished and inspected. This was no small task, for the ornament was big enough to cover his entire forehead and part of his trunk. The red velvet cloth, which was to be spread beneath the maharajah's throne on the elephant's back was cleaned and brushed.

Beside him stood the two dark brown jungle elephants. Pink lotus flowers were painted on their forelegs, and dancing cobras on their hind legs. Their youngest baby, a mischievous little fellow, was capering about and teasing the keepers. He was to be painted exactly like his parents, and in the parade the three of them were to walk behind the big elephant. . . .

The old sacred cow had her horns and hooves gilded. The ancient cloth with all the golden bells on it was tried on, though everyone knew it fitted her. . . .

After the noonday rest, the procession was formed up outside the palace. With bowed head, swaying his huge body to and fro on his solid legs, the big elephant stood and waited. . . .

First the drummers, who were to give the procession a

festive rhythm. After them, various regiments of the maharajah's soldiers in glittering uniform. Then a group of riflemen on white horses, and following them another group on black ones. Nobody remembered the big elephant, but he remembered himself, and went and took his place of his own accord.

The howdah was brought. The elephant had to kneel whilst it was lifted up and secured to his back. The high white steps on the small red wheels were pushed into position, so that the maharajah could use them to reach the howdah.

The rest of the parade was a mixture of war-chariots, huntsmen, horsemen with leopard skins over their backs, policemen, and all the costly palanquins and coaches that were to be found in the palace. When the whole procession had formed up, it reached twice round the palace.

At last the moment had come. The town clock struck four, the palace doors opened and the maharajah came out. All the gold and precious stones of the treasury adorned his white silk garments . . .

The maharajah strode across the square, mounted the white steps and took his place in the howdah on the elephant's back. The master of the ceremonies gave a signal to the drummers, and the procession moved off.

All along the route rows and rows of people stood as they were accustomed to do. They sat on balconies and roof tops and shouted, 'Long live His Highness, our good and divine ruler!'

from *Shanta*

# OCTOBER 25th

## Saint Crispin's Day

On Saint Crispin's Day, 1415, the battle of Agincourt was fought between the English, under King Henry V, and the

French. We can read about this battle in Shakespeare's play, *King Henry V*. The English army was small, wearied out with long marches, half starved, and racked with dysentery; and when, having crossed the river Somme, they found, facing them, a French army outnumbering them by five to one, and every man fresh, the Earl of Westmoreland exclaimed:

> 'O that we now had here
> But one ten thousand of those men in England
> That do no work today!'

But not so thought King Henry. If they were to die, he said, then the fewer they were, the less would be England's loss. But if they were to win the battle, as win they assuredly could and would – why then, the fewer the men, the greater the honour:

KING HENRY:

> This day is call'd the feast of Crispian:
> He that outlives this day and comes safe home,
> Will stand a-tiptoe when this day is nam'd,
> And rouse him at the name of Crispian:
> He that shall live this day, and see old age,
> Will yearly on the vigil feast his neighbours,
> And say, Tomorrow is Saint Crispian:
> Then will he strip his sleeve and show his scars,
> And say, These wounds I had on Crispin's day.
> Old men forget; yet all shall be forgot,
> But he'll remember with advantages
> What feats he did that day: then shall our names,
> Familiar in their mouths as household words –
> Harry the king, Bedford and Exeter,
> Warwick and Talbot, Salisbury and Gloster –
> Be in their flowing cups freshly remember'd.
> This story shall the good man teach his son;
> And Crispin Crispian shall ne'er go by,

From this day to the ending of the world,
But we in it shall be remembered, –
We few, we happy few, we band of brothers;
For he today that sheds his blood with me
Shall be my brother; be he ne'er so vile,
This day shall gentle his condition:
And gentlemen in England now a-bed
Shall think themselves accurs'd they were not here,
And hold their manhoods cheap, while any speaks
That fought with us upon Saint Crispin's day.
*King Henry V, Act IV, Scene 3.*

And so, having heartened his soldiers with these valiant words, King Henry led them into battle; and to victory.

# OCTOBER 31st

## Hallow E'en

Hey-how for Hallow e'en,
When all the witches are to be seen,
Some in black and some in green,
Hey-how for Hallow e'en!

This is the night when not only witches, but fairies, goblins and ghosts are abroad. The witches fly on broomsticks, or ride on the backs of cats. They go, as they did on Midsummer Eve, to meet the Devil on some high place. The Devil comes to the rendezvous riding on a goat. The goat carries a blazing torch between his horns to light up the revels. The Devil plays the bagpipes, the witches dance – altogether a merry occasion.

Here from Scotland is a warning to children:

> Hallow e'en will come, will come,
> Witchcraft will be set a-going,
> Fairies will be at full speed,
> Avoid the road, children, children.

For on this night, the Fairy Queen and all her court set out to ride about the world. If you listen, you will hear the faint jingle of the bridle bells, and the soft, very soft, and very swift *clip-clop* of galloping hoofs. And then suddenly, in a glimmering

132

mist, the whole company sweeps by you and is gone. And you are left wondering whether you are awake or dreaming.

Down through the years, Hallow e'en has been a night for giving parties, at which you play a game called Bobbing for Apples. The apples are put into a big tub of water. The players, hands behind backs, try to pick up an apple out of the tub with their teeth – and get well soused about the head and face in the process. Another game is played with nuts, and Hallow e'en sometimes goes by the name of Nut Crack Night. You whisper your lover's name and throw a nut into the fire. If it burns quietly, all is well. But if it cracks and bursts, your lover will not be true to you.

American and Canadian children have their own special observance for this night. It is called Trick'n and Treat'n, and here is a story about it:

# Trick'n and Treat'n

## *Christopher Floyd*

It was Hallow e'en night: the moon was full, the air was cold, and the trees were craggy. The figures of two demons could be seen treading up a winding lane. One was a scaly red demon with a long floppy tail; he might have been a dragon or a devil, or perhaps one of those huge prehistoric lizards you sometimes see in museums. Only he wasn't: for one thing he was only three foot six inches tall. And his companion, a black demon with wings like a bat, was even smaller.

Both were carrying sacks. Occasionally they'd take things out of the sacks and gobble them up with a grin. What do you think they were gobbling? Pieces of flesh? Magic herbs? No, not a bit of it! They were gobbling chocolate bars, toffee

133 .

apples, liquorice – all kinds of candy. You see, the figures weren't really demons at all, they were two brothers called Richard and Paul, who had dressed up as demons for Hallow e'en night. For it's an old custom in our part of the world that on Hallow e'en night all the children put on disguises, and go from door to door demanding 'trick'n treat'n'. This means 'Either you give me a treat, or I will play a trick on you'. Naturally most people prefer to give a treat, so that by the end of the evening, every child in the area has a big sack full of candy – enough to give him indigestion for a week.

So that's how it was that Richard and Paul were walking up a winding lane, dressed as demons, and carrying two sacks of candy. They had finished trick'n treat'n, and were now going home.

The way led through a deep wood, and the night seemed alive with creepy noises. An owl was hooting, dead leaves were rustling. Then suddenly a small voice began screaming, '*Yeeai! Yeeai! Yeeai!*'

'What was that?' Paul cried, jumping a foot into the air.

'Only a fox, silly,' said Richard. 'There is no need to be scared. We've only a little way to go now.'

'*Yeeai! Yeeai! Yeeai!*' cried the voice again. 'Gimme a treat! Trick or treat!'

'It *is* something!' whispered Paul, shivering all over.

'N-no, it isn't,' said Richard. 'How can it be? B-but let's run the rest of the way. Come on!'

Richard and Paul began running.

'I said *gimme a treat or I'll play a trick on you!*' the voice shrieked.

Richard and Paul stopped running and froze like statues. There *was* something! They looked all round: then suddenly they saw a very small blue creature come out of the woods into the lane. It was glowing slightly, otherwise they couldn't have seen it at all. What did it look like? Well, it looked something like Richard's costume, and something like Paul's

134

costume; but mostly it looked like a fat blue goblin. And that's what it was.

'Well?' said the goblin. 'What sort of treat are you going to give me? If you don't give me something I'll turn you into worms.'

'I d-don't know,' stammered Richard. 'What-what sort of treat do you want?'

'Whatever you have to give,' said the goblin, eyeing the sacks.

'There's a lot of candy in our sacks,' said Richard. 'We'll give you some of it, if – if you won't play a trick on us, and if you'll let us go home.'

'We'll see,' said the goblin. 'Give me a piece of candy.'

Richard took out a large toffee apple. The goblin suddenly sprang into the air and snatched the toffee apple out of Richard's hand. With one gulp he swallowed it whole. Now he looked even fatter.

'*Mmmm*,' he said, smacking his lips. 'Not bad!' He looked at Paul 'What's in the other sack?'

Paul took out a chocolate bar. The goblin snatched it out of his hand, swallowed it in one gulp, and spat out the wrapper.

'Fine!' he cried. 'Give me both sacks and I'll let you go. But first you must carry them to my hole. Come. This way!'

Richard and Paul followed the goblin through the wood till they came to a clearing. They knew that clearing well, they'd once made a fort there. But it looked different tonight: it was littered with sacks of candy.

'Yes!' cried the goblin. 'I've taken every single trick'n treat'n sack in this neighbourhood. I'll be able to feast for years and years! Come on now; put down your sacks and go home. And don't you dare tell anyone about me. If you do I'll change you into worms, I *will*!'

Richard and Paul looked at the goblin in dismay. But what could they do? Nothing. So they turned round and began to trudge home.

136

'The mean greedy beast!' cried Richard, as soon as they were out of earshot. 'We'll have to pretend we didn't get any candy from trick'n treat'n. What fools we'll look!'

'What an awful Hallow e'en!' Paul whimpered.

And so it would have been, had the story ended there. But it didn't. This is what happened:

Richard and Paul got home and went to bed as miserable as could be. But later that night, long after they'd fallen asleep, there came a tapping at their window. The tapping got louder and louder; till at last Richard woke up.

'Who's there?' he yawned.

'It's me! It's me!' a small voice cried. 'Get up! Get up!'

Richard got up and went to the window. And there, outside, he saw the blue goblin standing on the sill, with his face pressed against the pane. The goblin looked very fat.

'You again!' said Richard. 'What are you doing here? Haven't you taken enough for one night?'

The fat blue goblin gazed at Richard sadly. He didn't look at all frightening now. 'Y-yes,' moaned the goblin, 'I've taken too much. Much too much! I've eaten so many chocolates and toffees and liquorices that I'm too fat to get back down my hole. I'll be out all night, and if that happens, the morning sun will turn me into a snail! Oh, I'd hate to be a snail!' the goblin whimpered. 'Please help me! *Please!*'

Richard shook his head sternly. 'Why should I? You took all our candy!'

'I'll give it back,' wailed the goblin. 'All that's left of it.'

Richard looked at the goblin doubtfully. 'I don't see how I *could* help you,' he said. 'Even if I wanted to.'

'Yes, you could,' cried the goblin. 'You could wake your brother; then the two of you could go to the toolshed and borrow some spades. With the spades you can widen my hole enough for me to crawl out of the sunlight. Oh, please, please, *please!*' he began whimpering again. 'I don't want to be a snail and carry a great heavy load on my back all the time!'

137

Well, Richard went on looking at the fat little goblin, and strange to say he began to feel sorry for it. It looked very pathetic. So he said he would help and got dressed. Then he woke Paul.

Paul was suspicious. 'It's a trick!' he whispered.

'No, it's not,' said Richard. 'The goblin's speaking the truth. You can tell because it's shivering with fright.'

Paul still wasn't sure, but Richard was older than he was, so he agreed. The two boys went to the toolshed to get spades. They found the goblin waiting for them there.

'Hurry!' it gasped, 'Hurry! There are only a few hours to go. This way. Quick!'

They followed the wheezing goblin into the wood. Again it took them to the clearing, and again they could see the dozens of candy sacks. But this time they also saw a great litter of candy wrappers.

'No wonder you're so fat!' said Richard, gazing round.

The goblin moaned, and pointed to a tiny chink at the base of a tree trunk. 'That's my hole,' he said.

'What!' cried Paul, almost laughing. 'You'll never fit in there! Never!'

'I know,' whimpered the goblin. 'It was always a bit on the small side, even this evening when I was thin. But there's a chamber a few feet below ground, and if you can dig down to it, I can crawl in and bury myself out of the light. Then I can sleep off my full stomach.'

So Richard and Paul began digging. It was hard work, and they stopped often for a stick of candy. Soon they grew very tired, but the goblin kept hurrying them along. At last the earth they were digging caved in, and they knew they'd reached the chamber.

'Only just in time!' cried the goblin, pointing to the east, as he scrabbled through the earth into his chamber.

Richard and Paul looked round and saw a pale red tinge through the trees: it was almost dawn. Birds began chirping.

The goblin was well into his chamber now, so they shovelled some of the earth they'd already dug back on top, till the goblin was nearly covered.

'But what about all the candy?' asked Paul. 'What's going to happen to it?'

'Keep it,' the goblin mumbled. 'Keep it all. Only hurry! I don't want to be a snail!'

So the boys put on a few more shovelfuls, till nothing could be seen of the blue goblin and his chamber. Now the sky grew quite light, and they could see everything clearly. What a lot of candy there was left! The goblin had only eaten about a quarter of it.

'We can't keep all that,' said Paul.

'We'll keep what's ours, and maybe a bit more,' said Richard. 'And we'll divide the rest among the people he took it from.'

And that's what they did. So even though they went home very tired, what with being up most of the night and having to carry dozens of candy sacks home, they both felt very happy, when they went to bed next night. For not only had they got more candy than ever before, but also they'd been able to give everyone else some.

So it was a good Hallow e'en after all.

# Open House

In Scotland (and also in Brittany and Egypt) when people went to bed on Hallow e'en night, they would leave food on the table for the spirits of the dead to eat:

> It's the nicht atween the Saints and Souls
> When the bodiless gang aboot,
> And it's open house we keep this nicht
> For ony that may be oot.

139

# Calling Their Names

In Cornwall the ghosts of those drowned at sea are said to rise from the waves on Hallow e'en and call out their names.

## The Ghost Ship
## (A Cornish Story)

### *Ruth Manning-Sanders*

'After breakfast I coaxed a marvellous tale out of old John Lenine about the ghost ship,' said Sam.

'Tell us the tale, do!' I urged.

We pulled the settle and the big armchair up to the fire, and two of us sat in the chair, and three on the settle.

'Here goes then!' said Sam. 'You remember how Jan the Bad had drowned the old squire, Zach the Good, and taken the squire's house and lands? Well, it was soon after this that Jan the Bad was giving a Hallow e'en party in the banqueting hall. And they were carousing and dancing, and there were musicians up in the minstrels' gallery, and guise dancers (they're mummers that dress up and act daft) rushing about among the guests, and servants carrying round flagons of spiced wine. And so they went on until midnight. By that time the old tough guys were all roaring drunk, and the young unmarried ones, both men and women, decided they would play at telling their fortunes with rushes and ivy leaves.

'What you do is this. You make up a good clear fire. Then each of you touches the mantel stone with your forehead, and after that you mustn't speak a word or look behind you, but must go out, single file, and gather your ivy and rushes by moonlight. Then, when you come back, you each one touch the mantel stone with your forehead again. And then two at a time, a man and a woman, you throw a rush into the fire. If the rushes lean together as they burn, you two will be married, if they lean apart, you won't; and so you go on till the fate of all the party is known. Then the couples throw in one ivy leaf, and the number of cracks it gives as it burns is the number of months before they will be married. And, after that, each couple throws in two ivy leaves, and the number of cracks *they* give is the number of children they will have. It sounds a fool game, and anyone who decided to marry on the strength of a rush would be a mug, I should think. But anyway that's what they meant to do.

'So they all touched the mantel stone over the big hearth with their foreheads, and the stone was so high that the girls had to get on a chair to do it; and then they trooped out silently and single file across the court and into the drive. I've told you it was midnight and full moon, haven't I? "A bra' fine night without a cloud in the sky", old John said.

'I imagine the moon would be shining down over Mulberry Hill, and the drive would be white, and the thickets all crisscrossed with brightness and shadow, and the stream gleaming here and there under the trees, as I've seen it many a time. And so they went silently down the drive toward the gate, where they meant to gather rushes from the stream, and ivy leaves from the wall by the road.

'Very quiet the night was, and very bright. And then, just before they reached the gate, a white mist appeared from nowhere and covered the moon: and under the mist, over the top of Mulberry Hill, they saw the breaking waves of the sea.'

'*Waves?*' I echoed. 'Over the *top* of Mulberry Hill?'

'Yes, waves over Mulberry,' said Sam. 'Over the top of that high hill where we rode yesterday and looked down over all the countryside. The waves rose so high that their white spume seemed to be reaching for the hidden moon. The procession

141

stood for a moment rooted to the ground with horror. Then they began to run back toward the house, for the waves broke over the top of Mulberry and poured down the hillside in an avalanche, and across the fields, and in through Penmarth gates. The young men and women ran fast, but the sea came faster; and, as they dashed up the steps and through the great door, the waves were at their heels, the flying foam from the breakers was in their hair, and their stockings and their petticoats were drenched with spray.

'They slammed the great door and bolted it. They rushed into the banqueting hall, and there the drunks were sober, and the minstrels had ceased to play, for the roar of ocean sounded through all the house. The window panes shook with the thunder of the waves. And through the windows they could see the court awash in a rough misty sea. And on that sea was a ship, and in the ship was a crew of ghostly sailors, and at the prow stood the drowned old squire, Zach the Good, calling his name. And after him every sailor called his name; and then, with one voice, they all called together, 'Jan the Bad! Jan the Bad! Jan the Bad!' And nobody dared look or listen any more; they hid themselves in corners and stuffed their fingers in their ears; and when, after a long time, they did look again, the ship was gone and the sea was gone, the moonlight was bright in the courtyard, and Jan the Bad was stretched dead on the floor.

'There' – Sam drew a long breath – 'that's the tale I got this morning from old John Lenine.'

'My hat! And didn't you tell it well!'

Sam didn't reply to this compliment, he was too worked up.

from *Mystery at Penmarth*

November

# NOVEMBER 1st AND 2nd

## All Saints – All Souls

In former times the souls that had returned to earth on Hallow e'en were remembered and prayed for on the two following days, All Saints and All Souls: these two days being grouped together with Hallow e'en under the general name of Hallow Tide. And at Hallow Tide, since bonfires are always fun, bonfires blazed merrily. If you wanted an excuse for making a blaze, you could claim that you were lighting the souls on their way out of Purgatory; for meantime the church bells were ringing loud and clear to remind you that this was really a solemn occasion.

Then there were the soul-cakes; little spiced buns which you baked and sent as presents to your relatives. You had to bake plenty of these buns because children (and often grown-ups too) would be out *souling*: knocking at your door and singing their *Souling Song*:

> Soul, soul, for a souling cake,
> I pray, good missus, a souling cake.
> One for Peter, two for Paul,
> And three for Him who made us all;
> Up wi' the kettle, and down wi' the pan,
> Give us a big 'un, and we'll be gone.

And all the time the church bells rang and rang. They rang so persistently that they became a nuisance; and in the reign of Elizabeth I this constant clamour of bells at Hallow Tide had to be forbidden.

146

# NOVEMBER 5th

## Guy Fawkes Day

Remember, remember
The fifth of November,
Gunpowder treason and plot,
I see no reason
Why Gunpowder treason
Should ever be forgot.

All English children will heartily agree with the sentiment expressed in this rhyme; for throughout England the night of November 5th is a-glow with the blaze of bonfires and the glitter of fireworks – although the event which these bonfires and fireworks commemorate was not a happy one for those involved. For on this night:

Guy Fawkes and his companions
Did the scheme contrive
To blow the King and Parliament
All up alive!
But by God's providence, him they did catch,
With a dark lantern, lighting a match.
Hollo, boys! Hollo, boys! make the bells ring,
Hollo, boys! Hollo, boys! God save the King!

In the year 1605, a party of some thirteen Roman Catholic gentlemen, enthusiastic to restore the Catholic religion in England, formed a plot to do away with the King (James I) and the whole governing body of the country, by blowing them sky-high with gunpowder.

Parliament was to open on November 5th. On October 25th, Lord Monteagle, a Roman Catholic member of parliament received a mysterious letter:

'My Lord,

     . . . I have a care for your preservation. Therefore I would advise you, as you tender your life, to devise some excuse to shift your attendance to this parliament. For God and man hath concurred to punish the wickedness of this time . . . Retire yourself into your country, where you may expect this event in safety . . . they shall receive a terrible blow, this parliament, and yet shall not see who hurt them. This counsel can do you no harm, for the danger is passed as soon as you have burned this letter.'

But Lord Monteagle didn't burn the letter. He rode post haste up to London, and showed it to Mr Secretary Cecil and others of the King's Council. All the rooms and cellars under the Parliament House were immediately searched. In one cellar, a cellar stacked with wood and rented by a Roman Catholic called Percy, they found Mr Guy Fawkes, who gave his name as Johnson, and explained that he was Percy's servant. The searchers were a bit suspicious. However they went away. They did not then discover that under the stacked wood lay thirty-six barrels of gunpowder.

Now it was Guy Fawkes who had been chosen by the conspirators to light the slow fuse which was to ignite the gunpowder. At midnight on November 4th all was in readiness. As soon as Parliament assembled Guy Fawkes, who would be lurking in the cellar, was to light the fuse, and hurry away to a boat waiting on the Thames to carry him over to Flanders. In Flanders a regiment awaited the success of the plot to embark for England. And with the help of this regiment, and in the utter confusion which needs must follow the assassination of England's ruling body – King, Bishops, Lords, Commons and all – the conspirators would form a new government, and declare the country's return to the Old Faith. To them it was not a wicked but a holy undertaking, which must needs be well pleasing to God.

And so, at midnight on that 4th of November, Guy Fawkes betook himself to the fatal cellar, thinking there to await the moment when, Parliament being assembled, he should light his fuse. But he never did light that fuse. The searchers were there to meet him, and to go with him into the cellar. This time, flinging the piles of wood aside, they discovered the gunpowder, and on 'Mr Johnson' himself they found the dark lantern, a tinder box, and three matches. Mr Johnson was unrepentent. 'Had you but found me *inside* the cellar,' said he, 'I would have blown up you, myself, the House, and all.' He was bound, marched away, and put on trial. Still unrepentent, still maintaining that his name was Johnson, he was stretched on the rack, and tortured. Still he was silent. But the torturers knew their business. The pains grew more and more excruti-ating; till at last, unable to endure more, Guy Fawkes confessed, and gave the names of his associates. Some were killed in endeavouring to escape. The rest, including Guy Fawkes, were hanged.

And now yearly, all through the day on November 5th, parties of boys parade the streets, carrying with them a dummy of Guy Fawkes. The dummy is stuffed with straw or paper, dressed in any old clothes, and should properly wear a top hat. 'A penny for the old Guy! A penny for the old Guy!' shout the boys, rattling a money box. And pennies they get in plenty. The money is spent on fireworks, and when darkness falls and the bonfire is lit, the poor old Guy, perched a-top of the fire, goes up in flames: whilst round him flare and crackle the fireworks he has played his part in earning.

# The Fifth of November

## *P. L. Travers*

Daylight was fading as they crossed the road. By the Park railings Bert, the Match Man, was spreading out his tray. He lit a candle with one of his matches and began to draw pictures on the pavement. He nodded gaily to the children as they hurried through the gates.

'Now all we need,' the Sweep said fussily, is a clear patch of grass —'

'Which you won't get!' said a voice behind them. 'The Park is closed at 5.30.'

Out from the shadows came the Park Keeper, looking very belligerent.

'But it's Guy Fawkes' Day – the Fifth of November!' the children answered quickly.

'Orders is orders!' he retorted, 'and all days are alike to me.'

'Well, where can we let off the fireworks?' Michael demanded impatiently.

A greedy look leapt to the Keeper's eyes.

'You got some fireworks?' he said hurriedly. 'Well, why not say so before!' And he snatched the parcel from the Sweep and began to untie the string. 'Matches – that's what we need!' he went on, panting with excitement.

'Here,' said the Match Man's quiet voice. He had followed the children into the Park, and was standing behind them with his lighted candle.

The Park Keeper opened a bundle of squibs.

'They're *ours*, you know!' Michael reminded him.

'Ah, let me help you – do!' said the Keeper. 'I've never 'ad fun on Guy Fawkes' Day – never since I was a boy!'

And without waiting for permission, he lit the squibs at the Match Man's candle. The hissing streams of fire poured out, and pop, pop, pop, went all the crackers. The Park Keeper seized a Catherine Wheel, and stuck it on a branch. The rings of light began to turn, and sparkled on the air. And after that he was so excited that nothing could stop him. He went on lighting fuse after fuse as if he had gone mad.

Flower Pots streamed from the dewy grass and Golden Rain flowed down through the darkness. Top Hats burned for a bright short moment. Balloons went floating up to the branches; and Firesnakes writhed in the shadows. The children jumped and squeaked and shouted. The Park Keeper ran about among them like a large frenzied dog. And amid the noise and the sparkling lights the Match Man waited quietly. The flame of his candle never wavered as they lit their fuses from it.

'Now!' cried the Keeper, who was hoarse with shouting. 'Now we come to the rockets!'

All the other fireworks had gone. Nothing remained in the nobbly parcel except three long black sticks.

'No you don't!' said the Sweep, as the Keeper snatched them. 'Share and share. That's fair!' So he gave the Keeper one rocket and kept the others for himself and the children.

'Make way, make way!' cried the Keeper importantly, as he lit the fuse at the candle flame and stuck the stick in a hole in the ground.

Hissing and guttering, the spark ran along like a little golden thread. Then – whoop! went the rocket as it shot away. Up in the sky the children heard a small far-away bang. And a swirl of red-and-blue stars broke out and rained upon the Park.

'Oh!' cried the children. And 'Oh!' cried the Sweep. For that is the only word any one can say when a rocket's stars break out.

Then it was the Sweep's turn. The candle-light gleamed on his black face as he lit the fuse of his rocket. Then came a whoop and another bang, and white-and-green stars spread over the sky like the ribs of a bright umbrella. And again the watchers all cried 'Oh!' and sighed for sheer joy.

'It's our turn now!' cried Jane and Michael. And their fingers trembled as they lit the fuse. They pressed the stick down into the earth and stepped back to watch. The golden fire ran up the fuse. Whe-e-e-ew! Up went the rocket with a singing sound, up to the very top of the sky. And Jane and Michael held their breath as they waited for it to burst.

At last, far away and very faint, they heard a little bang.

Now for the stars, they thought to themselves.

But – alas! – nothing happened.

'Oh!' said everyone again – not for joy this time, but for disappointment. For no stars broke from the third rocket. There was nothing but darkness and the empty sky.

'Tricksy – that's what they are!' said the Sweep. 'There are some as just doesn't go off! Well, come on 'ome, all. There's no good staring. Nothing will come down now!'

'Closing Time! Every one out of the Park!' cried the Park Keeper importantly.

But Jane and Michael took no notice. They stood there watching, hand in hand. For their hopeful eyes had noticed something that nobody else had seen. Up in the sky a tiny spark hovered and swayed in the darkness. What could it be? Not the rocket, for that must have burned itself out long ago. And certainly, not a star, they thought, for the little spark was moving.

'Perhaps it's a special kind of rocket that has only one spark,' said Michael.

'Perhaps,' Jane answered quietly, as she watched the tiny light.

Even if there was only one spark they would watch till it went out. But strangely enough, it did not go out. In fact, it was growing larger.

'Let's get a move on!' urged the Sweep. And again the Park Keeper cried:

'Closing Time!'

152

'*A penny for the old Guy!*
*A penny for the old Guy!*'

But still they waited. And still the spark grew ever larger and brighter. Then suddenly Jane caught her breath. And Michael gave a gasp. Oh, was it possible – ? Could it be – ? they silently asked each other.

Down came the spark, growing longer and wider. And as it came, it took on a shape that was strange and also familiar. Out of the glowing core of light emerged a curious figure – a figure in a black straw hat and a blue coat trimmed with silver buttons – a figure that carried in one hand something that looked like a carpet-bag, and in the other – oh, could it be true? – a parrot-headed umbrella.

Behind them the Match Man gave a cry and ran through the Park Gates.

The curious figure was drifting now to the tops of the naked trees. Its feet touched the highest bough of an oak and stepped down daintily through the branches.

It stood for a moment on the lowest bough and balanced itself neatly.

Jane and Michael began to run and their breath broke from them in a happy shout.

'Mary Poppins! Mary Poppins! Mary Poppins!' Half-laughing, half-weeping, they flung themselves upon her.

from *Mary Poppins Opens the Door*

# NOVEMBER 30th, SAINT ANDREW'S DAY

## The 'Marvellous Pleasant Story' of Saint Andrew, the Bishop, and the Devil

You must know that there was a bishop who loved Saint Andrew above all other saints, and every day said prayers in his honour. This so annoyed the Devil that he determined to do the bishop a michief. So he turned himself into a most lovely lady, and the lovely lady came to the bishop's palace, and sent a message to the bishop, saying that she wished to confess.

'Then let her go to the priest appointed to hear confessions,' said the bishop.

But the lady answered that what she had to confess could only be told to the bishop himself, and so persistent was she that at last the bishop ordered her to be brought before him.

(Oh me, never had the bishop imagined that any human creature could be so beautiful – he was near to losing his wits just gazing at her!)

Well, well, she had some cock-and-bull story ready for the bishop. She was, she said, the daughter of a mighty king, who was determined to give her to a prince in marriage. But she, having devoted herself to piety, was equally determined to marry no man. And so, being threatened by the king, her father, to be put to the torture, she had fled to the bishop for protection.

Such beauty, such precious tears, such an angelic voice, such infamous ill-treatment of a saintly creature – *of course* the bishop would protect her! And he invited her to dine with him.

So the beautiful lady, otherwise the Devil, sat down to dine with the bishop and his company.

During the meal, the bishop paid her so much attention that the Devil 'perceived his advantage and began to increase in beauty more and more', until the poor bishop, quite overcome, 'conceived for her a greater affection than a bishop should'.

'Then a pilgrim smote at the bishop's gate, and though he knocked hard, they would not open to him. Then the pilgrim at the gate knocked louder, and the bishop grew less charitable and more polite, and asked the beautiful creature before him

155

whether it was her pleasure that the pilgrim should enter. And she desired that a question (which she would ask) should be put to the pilgrim, which if he could answer, he should be received, and if he could not, he should abide without, as not worthy to come in. And the company assented thereto.'

So the bishop sent a messenger to the pilgrim to ask the question. The question was this:

What is the distance from the bottomless pit unto the imperial heaven?

And when the messenger had asked the pilgrim this question, the pilgrim answered, 'Go to him that sent thee, and ask the question of *him*; because he measured the distance when he fell from heaven into the bottomless pit, and *I* never measured it.'

The messenger, sore afraid, fearfully told the pilgrim's answer to the bishop and all the others, who when they heard it were also sore afraid. Then forthwith the Devil vanished away from before their eyes. And the bishop repented and sent the messenger to bring in the pilgrim, but he could not be found. So the bishop assembled the people and told them what had happened, and required them to pray that it might be revealed who this pilgrim was that had delivered him from so great a peril: and the same night it was revealed to the bishop that it was Saint Andrew who had put himself into the habit of a pilgrim for the bishop's deliverance.

'Then began the bishop more and more to have devotion and remembrance of Saint Andrew than he had before.'

*The Golden Legend*

# American Thanksgiving Day

> O give thanks unto the lord, for he is good: for
> his mercy endureth forever.
>
> *Psalm 136*

In the year 1620 nineteen Puritan families set sail for America
in the *Mayflower*. On the 21st of December they settled in
Massachusetts at a place they called Plymouth, in memory
of the last English port they had touched. They staked and
laid out two rows of huts, but soon they had to face a long
hard winter of sickness and famine, when they 'knew not at
night where to have a bit for the morning.' And within their
first year they had to make seven times as many graves for
their dead as they did huts for their living.

However, dauntless in courage, they managed to till some
land and sow barley and Indian corn; and when these crops
were harvested they decided to set aside 'an especial day on
which to give especial thanks for all their mercies'.

So Governor Bradford, the leader of the colony, ordered
a day of thanksgiving, and sent out four men to hunt for meat.
They came back with plenty of turkeys, and on these they
feasted. The feast was joined by a Red Indian Chief and
ninety of his men. When the food was getting low, the Chief
sent four of his braves out hunting, and they returned with
five deer.

So these Puritans laboured on through the years, and were
joined by more and more Puritan emigrants: 'men driven
forth from their fatherland . . . by fear of God and the zeal
for godly worship'; and throughout New England it became
the custom every year to set aside a day after the harvest for
thanksgiving prayer and feasting. These Puritans disapproved
of Christmas as a day smacking of heathen idolatry, but a
harvest thanksgiving was another matter; and even the mince
pies which, when eaten on Christmas Day, were 'idolatries

in crust', were quite another matter, delicious and welcome fare, when eaten on Thanksgiving Day.

And then, more than a hundred years later, when America had severed her dependence on England, and become a free nation, President Washington issued a proclamation:

> 'To recommend to the people of the United States a Day of Public Thanksgiving and Prayer . . . Now therefore I do . . . assign Thursday, the Twenty Sixth of November next to be devoted by these States to the service of that great and glorious Being, who is the beneficent Author of all the good that is, that was, or will be.'

And, still later, after the American Civil War, President Lincoln issued yet another proclamation:

> 'The year that is drawing to its close has been filled with the blessings of fruitful fields and healthful skies. To these bounties, which are so constantly enjoyed that we are prone to forget the source from which they come, others have been added . . . It has seemed to me fit and proper that they should be solemnly and gratefully acknowledged as with one heart and voice by the whole of the American people. I do, therefore, invite my fellow citizens in every part of the United States, and also those who are at sea and those who are sojourning in foreign lands to set apart . . . the last Thursday of November next as a day of thanksgiving and praise to our beneficent Father who dwelleth in the heavens.'

# A Fable

## *Oliver Herford*

It was a hungry pussy cat
Upon Thanksgiving morn,
And she watched a thankful little mouse
That ate an ear of corn.

'If I ate that thankful little mouse,
 How thankful he should be,
When he has made a meal himself,
To make a meal for me!

'Then, with his thanks for having fed
And his thanks for feeding me –
With all his thankfulness inside –
How thankful *I* should be.'

Thus mused the hungry pussy cat
Upon Thanksgiving Day.
But the little mouse had overheard,
And declined (with thanks) to stay.

*Artful Antics*

# December

# Susan's Christmas Stocking

## *Alison Uttley*

Susan awoke in the dark of Christmas morning. A weight lay on her feet, and she moved her toes up and down. It was Christmas day. She stretched out her hand and found the knobbly little stocking, which she brought into bed with her and clasped tightly in her arms as she fell asleep again.

She awoke later and lay holding her happiness, enjoying the moment. The light was dim, but the heavy mass of the chest of drawers stood out against the pale walls, all blue like the snow shadows outside. She drew her curtains and looked out at the starry sky. She listened for the bells of the sleigh; but no sound came through the stillness except for the screech owl's call.

Again she hadn't caught Santa Claus. Of course she knew he wasn't real, but also she knew he was. It was the same with everything. People said things were not alive, but you knew in your heart they were: statues which would catch you if you turned your back were made of stone; Santa Claus was your own father and mother, the stuffed fox died long ago.

But suppose people didn't *know*! They hadn't seen that stone woman walk in Broomy Vale Arboretum, but she might, in the dark night. They hadn't seen Santa Claus and his sleigh, but that was because they were not quick enough. Susan had nearly caught things happening herself, she knew they only waited for her to go away. When she looked through the window into an empty room, there was always a guilty look about it, a stir of surprise.

Perhaps Santa Claus had left the marks of his reindeer and the wheels of his sleigh on the snow in front of the house. She had never looked because last year there was no snow, and the year before she had believed in him absolutely. She would go out before breakfast, and perhaps she would find two marks of runners and a crowd of little hoof-marks.

She pinched the stocking from the toe to the top, where her white suspender tapes were stitched. It was full of nice lumps and knobs, and a flat thing like a book stuck out at the top. She drew it out . . . it *was* a book, just what she wanted most. She sniffed at it, and liked the smell of the cardboard back with deep letters cut in it. She ran her fingers along like a blind man and could not read the title, but there were three words in it.

Next came an apple, with its sweet, sharp odour. She recognized it, a yellow one, from the apple chamber, and from her favourite tree. She took a bite with her strong, white little teeth and scrunched it in the dark.

It was delicious fun, all alone, in this box-like room, with the dim blue-and-white jug on the washstand watching her, and the pool of the round mirror hanging on the wall, reflecting the dark blue outside, and the texts, 'Thou God seest me', and 'Blessed are the Peacemakers', and 'Though your sins be as scarlet they shall be white as wool'. They could see all the things though she couldn't, and they were glad.

Next came a curious thing, pointed and spiked, with battlements like a tower. Whatever could it be? It was smooth like ivory, and shone even in the dark. She ran her fingers round the little rim and found a knob. She gave it a tug and a ribbon flew out – it was a tape measure to measure a thousand things, the trees' girths, the calf's nose, the pony's tail. She put it on her knee, and continued her search.

There was a tin ball that unscrewed and was filled with comfits, and an orange, and a sugar mouse, all these were easy to feel, a sugar watch with a paper face, and a chain of coloured ribbon, a dolls' chair and a penny china doll with a round smooth head. She at once named it Diana, after Diana of the Ephesians, for this one could never be an idol, being made of pot. She put it next to her skin down the neck of her nightdress, and pulled the last little bumps out of the stocking toe. They were walnuts, smelling of the orchards at Bird-in-Bush Farm, where they grew on great trees overhanging the wall, and a silver shilling, the only one she ever got, and very great wealth, but it was intended for the money-box in the hall. It was the nicest Christmas stocking she had ever had, and she hugged her knees up to her chin and rocked with joy. Then she put her hand under the pillow and brought out five parcels which made five separate lumps under her head. They were quite safe.

She heard the alarm go off in her father's room and Dan's bell go jingle-jangle. Five o'clock, plenty of time yet before the hoof-marks would disappear. The wind swished softly against the window, and thumps and thuds sounded on the stairs. She slept again with the doll on her heart and the tape measure under her cheek and the book in her hand.

from *The Country Child*

## The Shepherds' Hymn

### *Richard Crashaw*

We saw Thee in Thy balmy nest,
Young dawn of our eternal day;
We saw Thine eyes break from the East,
And chase the trembling shades away:
We saw Thee, and we blest the sight,
We saw Thee by Thine own sweet light.

Poor world, said I, what wilt thou do
To entertain this starry stranger?
Is this the best thou canst bestow –
A cold and not too cleanly manger?
Contend, the powers of Heaven and earth,
To fit a bed for this huge birth.

I saw the curl'd drops, soft and slow,
Come hovering o'er the place's head,
Off'ring their whitest sheets of snow,
To furnish the fair infant's bed.
Forbear, said I, be not too bold;
Your fleece is white, but 'tis too cold.

I saw th'obsequious seraphim
Their rosy fleece of fire bestow,
For well they now can spare their wings,
Since Heaven itself lies here below.
Well done, said I; but are you sure
Your down, so warm, will pass for pure?

No, no, your King's not yet to seek
Where to repose His royal head;
See, see how soon His new-bloom'd cheek
'Twixt mother's breasts is gone to bed!
Sweet choice, said we; no way but so,
Not to lie cold, yet sleep in snow.

Welcome—tho' not to those gay flies
Gilded i'the beams of earthly kings,
Slippery souls in smiling eyes –
But to poor shepherds, homespun things,
Whose wealth's their flocks, whose wit's to be
Well read in their simplicity.

Yet, when young April's husband show'rs
Shall bless the fruitful Maia's bed,
We'll bring the first-born of her flowers,
To kiss Thy feet and crown Thy head.
To Thee, dread Lamb! whose love must keep
The shepherds while they feed their sheep.

To Thee, meek Majesty, soft King
Of simple graces and sweet loves,
Each of us his lamb will bring,
Each his pair of silver doves:
At last in fire of Thy fair eyes,
Ourselves become our own best sacrifice.


## The Birds

### *Percy Dearmer*

From out of the wood did a cuckoo fly,
Cuckoo,
He came to a manger with joyful cry,
Cuckoo!
He hopped, he curtsied, round he flew,
And loud his jubilation grew,
Cuckoo, cuckoo, cuckoo.

A pigeon flew over Galilee,
Vrercroo,
He strutted, and cooed and was full of glee,
Vrercroo,
And showed with jewelled wings unfurled

His joy that Christ was in the world,
Vrercroo, vrercroo, vrercroo.

A dove settled down upon Nazareth,
Tsucroo,
And tenderly chanted with all his breath
Tsucroo,
'O you,' he cooed, 'so good and true,
My beauty do I give to you –
Tsucroo, Tsucroo, Tsucroo.'

from *The Oxford Book of Carols*

## Lullay My Liking

Lullay my liking, my dear Son, my sweeting,
Lullay, my dear heart, mine own dear darling!

I saw a fair maiden
Sitten and sing:
She lullèd a little child.
A sweete lording:
Lullay, my liking, my dear Son, my sweeting,
Lullay, my dear heart, mine own dear darling!

Angels bright they sang that night
And saiden to that child
'Blessed be Thou, and so be she
That is so meek and mild.'
Lullay, my liking, my dear Son, my sweeting,
Lullay, my dear heart, mine own dear darling.

Pray we now to that child,
And to His mother dear,
God grant them all His blessing,
That now maken cheer!
Lullay, my liking, my dear Son, my sweeting,
Lullay, my dear heart, mine own dear darling!

*15th century carol*

# The Christmas Crab Apples

## *Ruth Manning-Sanders*

The demon Rubizal lived in the mountain. He was a mischievous one! He played tricks on people. He plagued the
wicked and the proud. He put horns on their heads; he gave
them pigs' snouts, and asses' tails. But he had a kind heart.

Many a poor peasant found money in his pocket, put there by Rubizal. And if he should meet a tired old woman, a long way from home, staggering under a bundle of faggots – puff! Rubizal blew out his cheeks: and the tired old woman found herself seated in comfort by her own fireside, with some of the faggots she had been gathering already blazing on the hearth.

Well, one bitter cold day, just before Christmas, Rubizal gave a hop, skip and jump down from his mountain into the valley. The ground was covered with snow, and trudging along through the snow towards Rubizal came a peasant, very ragged, very thin, and blue with cold. Under his left arm the peasant was carrying a little fir tree, and under his right arm he was carrying a bundle of ivy and holly twigs; and he was looking about him in a worried kind of way.

'What do you seek, my friend?' says Rubizal.

'Oh sir,' says the peasant, 'I am looking for crab apples. Today is Christmas Eve, and after Christmas Eve comes Christmas Day. I am a widower with seven little children, and I would make the time merry for them if I could. I have dug up this little tree; and as you can see, I have some ivy and some holly to decorate it. But I have no money to buy toys or pretty trifles to hang on the tree; and I thought if I could find a few crab apples to gay it up – well, the children would like that. And they could eat the little apples afterwards for a bit of a treat like. Though it would be but a sour feast, when all's said. But there, children will eat most anything . . . But it seems no crab apples grow hereabouts.'

'I know where there is a crab apple tree,' said Rubizal. 'Come!' And he took the peasant into a little wood. In the middle of the little wood was a little crab apple tree. (Well, of course Rubizal had just magicked it there.) The tree was bare of leaves, but there were still small apples hanging on it: not very bright, not very rosy, but still – apples.

The peasant, all joyful, set down his bundles, filled his

pocket with the little apples, picked up his bundles again.

'Goodbye, and thank you, sir,' says he.

'Goodbye,' says Rubizal. 'A happy Christmas to you!'

'The same to you, sir!' The peasant turned to go home.

'Love to the children!' Rubizal called after him.

'Whose love shall I say, sir?' says the peasant.

'Oh, just a merry old fellow's,' says Rubizal. And he laughs.

The peasant trudged off across the snow. Rubizal gave a jump. There he was, back on his mountain top.

That night, when he had put the children to bed, the peasant filled a box with earth, and planted the Christmas tree in it. He fastened a tallow candle to the top of the tree, and decorated the branches with ivy and holly. Then, very carefully, he threaded some wire through the top of each little apple, and hung the apples on the tree.

'And it does look real festive,' said the peasant to himself, as he stood back to admire his work. 'Though I could wish the apples were a bit more colourful.'

On Christmas morning, when the children saw the tree, they jumped and shouted. They took hands and danced round the tree. And when evening came, and the peasant lit the tallow candle, the ivy glittered and the red holly berries shone, and it seemed that even the little apples looked brighter.

How the children clapped their hands and danced and shouted:

> 'Oh how pretty! Oh how pretty!
> We've got a tree,
> A pretty, pretty tree,
> We've got a tree, the prettiest of all!'

And there they were, hopping and skipping and turning head over heels.

'But we mustn't forget the gentleman who found the apples,' said the peasant. 'He sent you his love.'

'No, we won't forget him!' cried the children, 'Who was he?'

171

'Just a merry old fellow,' said the peasant. 'Or so he told me. But the way he spoke, he seemed to me like some great lord.'

'Thank you, thank you, great lord!' shouted the children.

It was a merry evening, though they had nothing but cabbage soup and rye bread for supper.

'And when may we eat the little apples?' asked the children.

'Not till Twelfth Night,' said the peasant. 'That's the day we must take down the tree.'

So, for twelve days, the tree stood in its box of earth in the kitchen. The ivy looked a bit more shrivelled every day, and the holly berries dropped off one by one. The grease from the tallow candle, which of course had burned itself out on Christmas night, lay in patches on the withering leaves: but surely, surely, the little apples were growing every day rosier and bigger! Yes, there was no doubt about it, they *were* rosier, and they *were* bigger. By Twelfth Night they were so big that the branches on the tree bowed under their weight.

'I don't understand it,' muttered the peasant, as he carefully cut the wires and piled the heavy apples on a dish.

'Seems to me half an apple each will be enough for tonight,' says he. 'And they'll last you longer that way.'

'No, no, a whole one each!' cried the children.

'Well, half to begin with, anyway,' said the peasant. And he took a knife and began to halve one of the apples.

The knife cut into the juicy flesh: then it grated on something hard and stuck. What could it be? The peasant turned the apple upside down, and cut again. But again the knife stuck. 'There's something – queer about this apple,' muttered the peasant. And he put down the knife and wrenched the apple in two with his hands.

Oh! Oh! Oh! What do you think? Out of that apple tumbled six big rubies. Yes, the pips of that apple were precious stones.

'It's – it's witchcraft, it's a Twelfth Night dream, that's

173

'What do you seek, my friend?'
says Rubizal.

what it is!' gasped the peasant. And his hands trembled as he took up another apple and halved it.

It was no dream: the pips of this second apple were shimmering pearls.

And so it went on: the peasant halving apple after apple, and every apple pip a jewel: diamonds, sapphires, pearls, emeralds and rubies. When all the apples were halved, there on the kitchen table lay a gleaming heap of jewels; and even the children, as they munched away at the most delicious fruit they had ever tasted, were awed into silence.

It was a long time before they any of them went to bed. And the peasant couldn't sleep. He turned and tossed, thinking of that pile of jewels. 'It's the fairies up to their Twelfth Night tricks,' said he to himself. 'In the morning all those precious stones will be gone.'

But they weren't gone. The fairies had nothing to do with it. It was a Christmas gift from the demon Rubizal.

So the peasant sold the jewels and bought a farm. Everything prospered with him and his children. No more meagre suppers of cabbage soup and rye bread for them! And each year, before they sat down to their Christmas feast, the happy peasant-turned-farmer gathered his children and his workpeople about him, raised his glass, and said, 'Here's a health to the Merry Old Fellow! May we never forget his goodness, whoever he may be!'

And 'A health to the Merry Old Fellow!' cried all in chorus.

Did they hear a chuckling laugh somewhere outside in the snowy darkness? Perhaps they did, perhaps they didn't.

retold from *A Bohemian Legend*

# Christmas Under the Indian Sun

## *Jon and Rumer Godden*

Christmas in Narayangunj was not like Christmas anywhere
else. To begin with, for our family, there could be no ordinary
Christmas shopping. Everything had to be bought through
our mail order catalogues though now and then a box-wallah
(pedlar) came, sent out from a shop in Calcutta.

It made a stir when a box-wallah came up the drive, carrying
his box on his head, and was invited on to the verandah to
show his stock. Pinned inside the lid were cards of buttons,
cards of hairslides, ribbons, needlebooks, while the trunk itself
was filled with lengths of cheap cloth, household linen, towels,
tablecloths, doilies and handkerchiefs – dull things to us. The
tray, though, held a fascinating motley, everything from combs
to pincushions, pencil boxes and crayons, cheap fountain pens,
tape measures that sprang back when they were pulled out
and small cheap toys. 'You don't want those,' Aunt Mary
said, as we picked up different things, but we did want them,
perhaps only for the sake of buying. None of us though had
much money, and very often the box-wallah packed up and
went away without having sold anything to any of us.

There was no decorating of house and rooms; Mam did
not like paper chains, and holly and ivy were far away from
Narayangunj as were Christmas trees; the only one we ever
saw was at the Club party. Fa's idea of the Christmas holiday
was to go away on a duck shoot.

'That man's never happy unless he's killing something,'
said Aunt Mary, which was of course not quite true. We
hated to see the small soft bodies, their heads aligned in the
shooting brace as they were cast down on the verandah when
he came back from one of his shooting expeditions, but then
we, as did Aunt Mary too, enjoyed game pie, wild duck, snipe

on toast. A duck shoot though could be a holocaust and Christmas was one time when Fa did not get his way; he was defeated by us children. Our idea, as with most children everywhere, was to have Christmas at home and as exactly like all other Christmases there as it could be.

It began conventionally enough on Christmas Eve with the hanging up of stockings, long coloured cotton ones borrowed from our dancing fancy dresses. The sight of their knobbed shape hung on a ribbon from our bedrails meant that Christmas Day was here at last, but usually we woke so early with excitement that, in the dim dawn light, the ribbons did not show their Christmas red and we had to lie for what seemed hours, only looking at our stockings, until Hannah came along the verandah and we were allowed to jump up and claim them.

Morning tea was early because on Christmas Day we did what we did not do in Narayangunj on any other day in the year: we went to church, though not in a church, in the Masonic lodge to which a Church of England padre came in a white cassock and khaki topee. The Christmas service always seemed queerly out of place in the bare whitewashed Masonic hall that still had its old pull-punkahs, and it meant little to sing *Once in Royal David's City* and *Hark the Herald Angels Sing* at eight o'clock in the balm and sun of a Bengal cold weather morning. Christmas for us did not mean a crib and carols; it was tangled in our minds with the coral colours of pink oleanders, in full bloom then, and with the scent of violets – the Masonic gardener grew pots of them – and with the stiff little buttonholes, one rose or one marigold in a frill of maiden-hair fern which he presented to all the congregation as we came out. 'Hoping for bak-sheesh,' said Fa.

There were two highlights in our Christmas Day: the first was the family present-giving when, after an almost unbearable wait shut in Fa's room while Mam, Aunt Mary and Fa hid the presents, we were let out to look for them all over the garden. Parcels would be up trees, in the middle of bushes, behind bamboos, under flowerpots, tied to the swing, and when, breathless, we had collected them all, there would be an orgy of wonder as we opened them. Presents were not wrapped in fancy papers then, nor tied with ribbons, but the plain brown paper and string was quite as exciting. This treasure hunt, though, did not come directly after breakfast; there was a long wait to be gone through first, a ceremony for which we had to be washed and combed, the two hours or more for the getting and the giving of dollies.

A 'dolli' was not a doll; the name came from the Hindu word 'dali', meaning an offering or gift. It had become a custom, and custom had built up a ritual for it; the dollies were not handed over in the offices; they were presented, and presented with Indian courtesy, which meant that every giver had to call personally and make his salaams.

The salaam has become a catch phrase from old Anglo–India, but it has a deeply courteous meaning; an Indian does not shake hands unless he is westernized; he dislikes public contact with other people. An Indian parent will lead a child, not by holding its hand but delicately, with a finger and thumb, by the wrist. Instead of a handshake, he uses the namashkar, the graceful movement that means 'to take other's dust upon you', hands joined together as if in prayer and raised to the forehead or the breast according to the rank or honour of the person saluted. Indian children touch their parents' feet in homage. It is always an act of greeting and respect and from early morning, on Christmas Day, the contractors, merchants and head office staffs had been driving about Narayangunj and crossing the river to call on their Christian employers and clients.

Fa and Mam received, as it were, on the roomy front verandah where chairs were arranged, a carpet spread. Azad Ali announced each visitor in turn; perhaps it would be one of Fa's own babus resplendent in snow-white muslin shirt and dhoti, coloured socks and sock suspenders, patent leather pumps; or it might be a merchant, usually rich and dressed in a cream silk achkan, marigold-coloured turban, a fresh scarlet tika mark on his forehead.

The merchants would often bring their children, little boys and girls in European clothes but wearing ear-rings and hats like velvet pillboxes embroidered with gold. We would be told to take them and show them our toys but they were usually too shy to come with us and would only stare with their big dark eyes.

The ritual was always the same: Fa was garlanded, then Mam, but after a minute the long necklaces of jessamine or marigold flowers were taken off and coiled on a tray held by Abdul – Abdul of course had to be in this – and as time went on the pyramid of garlands grew into a scented mountain. The caller was seated and lemonade, fruit-juice and sweets were offered and, usually, refused. Five minutes were then spent in conversation, during which the baskets were carried in, put down at Fa's feet and politely ignored until the moment arrived in which to thank for them.

Dollies were always in light round baskets of the sort coolies use, but now decorated with flowers and sheets of coloured paper. Sometimes there was only one, sometimes two or three, their number depending on the richness of the giver and the importance of Fa's patronage to him; sometimes it was in genuine gratitude for help in the past year, but the giver knew, as Fa knew, as every one in India knew, that there was a code of strict limitation on the cost.

In the old days dollies were often bribes, and such fabulous bribes that no government employee was allowed to accept them. This suspicion of bribery still hung over them and any-thing gold or silver, even children's bangles, was immediately handed back; there could be none of the exquisite gauze and gold thread saris or scarves that came from Benares; a bottle of whisky or a length of plain silk was the utmost limit.

The foundation was always fruit: red apples from Kulu,

bananas – sometimes a whole stem of them was carried and set beside the basket as an extra – papayas, pommelloes like big pink-fleshed grape-fruit, tangerines in silver paper, boxes of dates and nuts. To one side would be a Christmas cake, florid with shop icing, which we thought wonderful compared to our home-made one. There would be a box of chocolates tied with ribbon, sometimes four boxes of chocolates, one for each of us though we would not be allowed to keep them, and there were Indian sweets, jillipis or sāndesh. Crackers and toys were poised on top. We children had to thank for them; the caller airily waved his hand and said, 'They are nothing, nothing,' though they must have cost him many rupees; he then made way for the next visitor and went on to pay his next call. For the Marwaris and babus it must have been an arduous and expensive morning, for us children it was a training in patience, obedience and generosity. Though Fa got dozens of dollies we were never allowed to have any of the things in them for ourselves. 'As well as a time for getting, Christmas is a time for giving,' said Mam and, 'You must not only learn to give, you must love giving.'

'Oh, *Mam* !'

'Yes,' said Mam firmly and as soon as the last tikka-gharri or carriage had driven away, we were all four sent into the dining-room where Hannah and Abdul had been busy un-packing the baskets and arranging pyramids of fruit, platters of sweets, rows of cakes, piles of crackers on the dining-room table; the toys were heaped on the floor; the empty cracker boxes set ready. While this was going on, a shuffling and rustling, whispering, giggling and sniffling had been growing on the back verandah. The noise grew louder and louder until Azad Ali clapped his hands as a signal and the droves of the servants' children came in, all of them including the dhobi's clan now mysteriously swelled to double size, but Mam never sent any of the small gatecrashers away. Some of the children we knew because they lived in the compound; some, like

179

Azad Ali's, came only at Christmas; some were enemies –
there had been scuffles and ambushes; some were friends –
Nitai's son could fly our kites better than we could. But now
it was as if we had never met before; we of the back verandah
were quite as ceremonious as our elders of the front and though
there were, of course, no garlands, the children gave us salaams
which we gravely returned.

The protocol was strict: Azad Ali's big girl and small boys
stood nearest the table, they in clean shirts and trousers, she
in salwar-kameeze, the loose tunic and trousers, with a little
gauze head or breast scarf worn by Muslim and up-country
girls. Govind's and the other gardeners' children stood apart
because they were Brahmins, the girls exquisite in saris,
jessamine flowers in their hair, the boys in clean muslin, patent
leather shoes on their bare feet. The dhobi's children were
everywhere, some of them dressed only in a charm string and
short cotton jacket that left their rice-swollen stomachs and
private parts bare. The babies wore nothing at all except
charm strings. Far over by the door stood Nitai's son and behind
him the smaller boy who came to pick up the crow corpses.

This protocol was not of Fa's and Mam's seeking – were
we not often companions of Nitai's boy? – but we knew that
now, as untouchable, he must keep apart, just as we knew that
the gardener's children must not be given fruit or cakes or
sweets: they would not be allowed to eat them because non-
Brahmini hands had touched them, non-Brahmini shadows
had fallen on them; not only non-Brahmini, untouchable
because by Hindu ruling we, as western children, were un-
touchables as well.

We parted first with the fruit and nuts; these were tied
swiftly into the corners of saris or dhotis or collected by the
dhobi's wife into an old pillow case. (The dhobi's wife always
fascinated us because she had elephantiasis. We stared at her
gargantuan feet and ankles.) Then each of the children was
given an empty cracker box or its lid to hold. These were filled

with sweets; the boxes of chocolates were ripped open or given whole to a family. Then the Christmas cakes were allotted and this was done in the unfair way of the world: the largest and best cakes to the richest children, the worst to the neediest, but Mam always kept a collection of inconspicuous pink-iced cakes to help fill the maws of the dhobis and their friends. At last came the moment for which everyone was really waiting, the distribution of the toys. Here again the rich had the best: Azad Ali's daughter the most splendiferous doll, the dhobi children the collection of celluloids, but immediately after came the crackers as consolation. Crackers were always divided equally.

People say that crackers are expensive nonsense; they should have seen those children with them. 'A-aah! A-aah! Aie! Aie!' Murmurs broke out all over the room. The big eyes grew bigger, brown faces broke into smiles; the small brown hands holding the cardboard box trays trembled. Those crackers would be kept long after the things inside them had been taken out, the gaudy fringed papers, the least tinselled star be made a treasure. Then the ritual was finished. In a few minutes the last child had salaamed and scurried away; the baskets were picked up empty. Once again everything was gone.

'Can't we keep that *darling* little doll? One little basket of cooking pots? One box of chocolates?' But we never could. The answer was always the same and, however reluctantly, we had always to be complete little Lady Bountifuls, though Hannah sometimes had literally to prise a drum of Turkish Delight or a box of chocolates out of Rose's hand.

One set of presents, though, Fa and Mam could not refuse for us. Of all the servants, excepting perhaps Hannah, we loved Guru best, and he loved us, all four of us, how much we were to discover one Christmas day. To an Indian servant with his pittance of pay, every anna, every pice, is precious, probably vital, yet on that Christmas morning Guru appeared with four long boxes made of that peculiarly thin, matt-white and rather damp cardboard of which doll boxes used to be made; inside them were four, large, jointed, and elaborately-dressed dolls; their clothes were glued on, not sewn, their shoes were paper, their hair ended under their chip straw hats, and their eyes were fixed, not opening and shutting, in fact they were cheap dolls but not for Guru; they must have cost him at least his whole month's wages. Even Rose was struck dumb and made none of her usual blunt comments, while, 'He must have spent a *pound*!' said Nancy. To her a pound was an enormous sum of money. Fa and Mam were in a quandary; they could not make the money up to Guru, that would have been an insult and would have made nonsense of his present, but 'What is he to live on?' asked Mam. It is good to think that we had the grace to treat these dolls with reverence, partly because of Guru and partly because they were not the sort of dolls one could play with, being too artificial, and they stayed intact for many a long day.

Christmas is usually marked by a feast of eating and drinking, but not for us: there were no traditional hams in Narayangunj, no turkeys; we had a goose which we children would not eat; it had been tethered near the cookhouse for weeks and we had fed it, unknowingly helping to fatten it. Mam and Aunt Mary made a Christmas cake which we all stirred – it was iced with home-made-looking icing; they made mince pies and we had a Christmas pudding, tinned; but the only unusual treat, the one to which we looked forward, was the crystallized fruit put on the luncheon table as if for a dinner party; we were allowed six crystallized cherries each and one large fruit; it was agonizing to choose between a candy pink pear, a dark greengage, or one of the deep gold globes of peaches.

After lunch it was time to dress for the Club party, the second highlight of the day.

from *Two Under the Indian Sun*

# DECEMBER 31st, NEW YEAR'S EVE

## Hogmanay or Cake Day in Scotland

### *R. Chambers*

In country places in Scotland, and also in the more retired
and primitive towns, it is customary on the morning of the
last day of the year, or Hogmanay, for children to get themselves swaddled in a great sheet, doubled up in front, so as to
form a vast pocket, and then go along the streets in little bands,
calling at the doors for an expected dole of oaten-bread. In

expectation of the large demands thus made on them, house-wives busy themselves for several days beforehand, in pre-paring a suitable quantity of cakes. The children, on coming to the door, cry:

'Hogmanay,
Trollolay!
Get up, good housewife, and shake your feathers,
And dinna think that we are beggars;
For we are bairns come out to play,
Get up and gie's our hogmanay.
My feet's cauld, my shoon's thin;
Gie's my cakes, and let me rin.'

It is no unpleasing sight, during the forenoon, to see the children going laden home, each with his large apron bellying out before him, stuffed full of cakes, and perhaps scarcely able to waddle under the load.

from *The Book of Days*

## Between the Old Year and The New (Fortune Telling)

At midnight, on New Year's Eve, shut your eyes, open your Bible and place the forefinger of your right hand at random on the page. Then open your eyes and read the words on which your finger rests. If the words are hopeful, your luck in the New Year will be good. If baneful, so will your fortune be.

Or, if you are an unmarried girl, you may wash your vest before you go to bed, and hang it over a chair to dry. Then get into bed; and if you can stay awake long enough, your future husband will come into the room and turn the vest. If no one comes, then alas! It's maiden now, and maiden ever.

# Burning the Bush

## F. Kilvert

I sat up till midnight to watch the Old Year out, and the New Year in. The bells rang at intervals all the evening, tolled just before the turn of the night and the year, and then rang a joyous peal, and rang on till one o'clock. After I had gone to bed, I saw from where I lay a bright blaze sprung up in the fields beyond the river, and I knew that they were keeping up the old custom of Burning the Bush at New Year's Day in the morning. From the hill above the village . . . the whole valley can be seen early on New Year's morning alight with fires burning the bush.

# Ring Out Wild Bells

## Alfred Tennyson

Ring out, wild bells, to the wild sky,
The flying cloud, the frosty light:
The year is dying in the night;
Ring out wild bells, and let him die.

Ring out the old, ring in the new,
Ring, happy bells, across the snow,
The year is going, let him go;
Ring out the false, ring in the true.

185

Ring out the grief that saps the mind,
For those that here we see no more,
Ring out the feud of rich and poor,
Ring in redress to all mankind.

Ring out a slowly dying cause,
And ancient forms of party strife;
Ring in the nobler modes of life,
With sweeter manners, purer laws.

Ring out the want, the care, the sin,
The faithless coldness of the times;
Ring out, ring out, my mournful rhymes,
But ring the fuller minstrel in.

Ring out false pride in place and blood,
The civic slander and the spite;
Ring in the love of truth and right,
Ring in the common love of good.

Ring out old shapes of foul disease;
Ring out the narrowing lust of gold:
Ring out the thousand wars of old,
Ring in the thousand years of peace.

Ring in the valiant man and free,
The larger heart, the kindlier hand;
Ring out the darkness of the land,
Ring in the Christ that is to be.

from *In Memoriam*

# Acknowledgements

The publishers would like to thank the following publishers and trustees for their kind permission to reproduce copyright material:

Angus & Robertson and William Morrow for 'A Chinese Boy's New Year' from *The Gatekeeper's Son* by E. F. Lattimore.

George Allen & Unwin and Macmillan (New York) for an extract from *Daily Life in Russia Under the Last Tzar* by H. Troyat.

Ward Lock for 'Shrove Tuesday' from *The Wonder Book of Children of All Nations* edited by Harry Golding.

The Bodley Head for 'Pancake Day at Great Pagwell' from *The Incredible Adventures of Professor Branestawm* by Norman Hunter.

The Bodley Head for 'The Easter Hare' from *To Read and to Tell* compiled by Norah Montgomerie.

William Heinemann for 'Easter in Athens' from *A Window on Greece* by Barbara Whelpton.

H. W. Wilson for 'Children's Egg Rolling in the United States' based on *The American Book of Days* by George William Douglas.

W. W. Norton for 'The Bright Weather Festival' from *A Chinese Childhood* by Chiang Yee.

Oxford University Press for 'May Day' from *Lark Rise to Candleford* by Flora Thompson.

The Hogarth Press and William Morrow for 'A Village Peace Festival' from *Cider with Rosie* (American title: *The Edge of Day*) by Laurie Lee.

187